Introducing Health Care in Times Past

OTHER BOOKS BY IAN WALLER

Published by Family History Books

Family History Research Challenges and How to Solve Them
Introducing Manorial Records
Introducing Nonconformist Records

Published by the Society of Genealogists

My Ancestor was an Agricultural Labourer
My Ancestor was in the Royal Navy
My Ancestor was a Leather Worker
My Ancestor was a Mormon

All titles are available from www.familyhistorybooksonline.com

Introducing Health Care in Times Past

How our ancestors coped with illness and death

Volume 1: Medical Practices, Professions and Pioneers

Ian H Waller FSG FGRA

Published by

Family History Books
the publishing imprint of the Family History Federation
a registered charity number 1038721

P.O. Box 62 Sheringham, Norfolk NR26 9AR

ISBN: 9781916599055

First published 2024

Family History Books is the trading name of the
Federation of Family History Societies (Services) Ltd

Typeset by Chapter One Book Design

Printed by Henry Ling Limited
The Dorset Press
Dorchester DT1 1HD

IMPORTANT INFORMATION

The vast extent of the original text and its contents could not be contained successfully in one book alone. There is so much information within 172,000-odd words that the publishers, in agreement with the author, made the decision to present this comprehensive text as a series of four volumes under a single main title.

Each volume has a subtitle which clearly refers to its specific contents. The four volumes are:

Volume 1   Medical Practices, Professions and Pioneers
Volume 2   Diseases, Remedies, Epidemics and Accidents
Volume 3   Births, Deaths, Funerals and Mental Illness
Volume 4   Military Medical Care

For the benefit of readers, an indication of what is covered in each volume is shown below.

Volume 1 describes how medicine evolved through the centuries. It discusses various medicinal practices by *wise women and witches* in medieval times through to *quacks*, *apothecaries* and then how health care became more prioritised and organised with trained doctors, nurses and others. There are chapters on different kinds of hospitals from almshouses and poor law infirmaries to the more modern hospitals of today. It also discusses some famous medical pioneers and developments in heath care from very basic medical equipment to vaccinations and penicillin.

Volume 2 covers diseases through the centuries in some detail ranging from *evil spirits in the head* in medieval times, various epidemics and hereditary diseases to childhood disorders. The section on accidents at work covers agricultural work to the Industrial Revolution and much more. This volume also examines some unusual cures and remedies, especially those in earlier times, and uncovers some myths and folklore too.

Volume 3 is all about birth, death and funerals. It covers how our ancestors dealt with childbirth centuries ago from basic care in medieval times to Victorian trends – and includes some odd superstitions about childbirth too. As sure as night follows day, death follows birth and the causes of death are examined in detail in this volume. This volume includes extensive details about funerals and how they have changed over the years. The volume ends by discussing the asylum system and how our ancestors dealt with mental illnesses.

Volume 4 covers all aspects of medical care in the military from the Crusades in the twelfth century, the Battle of Agincourt, the Napoleonic and Crimean Wars through to the extensive care dealing with casualties in both world wars. The methods of transporting the wounded in the war zones are examined including the various military and volunteer groups that were involved such as naval nursing, volunteer aid detachments, the British Red Cross and many others. There are also extensive details of medicine, heath care and surgery at sea. This volume ends with the transition to the NHS and details about the Wellcome Institute for the History of Medicine.

VOLUME 1

Medical Practices, Professions and Pioneers

ACKNOWLEDGMENTS

This series of books has been some years in the making with many weeks spent researching in archives and libraries including some specialist ones.

I wish to thank Family History Books who agreed to publish this extensive study. I couldn't have done it without the splendid editorial team and their facilitator, Jacqui Simkins, who steered everyone calmly through some tricky decisions.

No author can work without a good proofreader. I have been fortunate to work with Suzie Woodward for some years, and on this series she also did extensive work as copy editor. Her forensic eye for detail and all her helpful suggestions have been invaluable and I extend my warmest thanks and appreciation for all her hard work – and her patience!

Ian Waller,
2024

CONTENTS

TIMELINE

The following timeline highlights some of the more significant events which took place through the centuries.

12th cent.	During the Crusades doctors began using Arabian medicine to treat wounds and disease
1173	The established infirmary of St Mary Overie was renamed St Thomas' Hospital, London
1267	Spectacles and magnifying glasses using convex lenses to correct vision were developed
1348–9	The Black Death sweeps through Britain
1415	Battle of Agincourt
1489	Leonardo da Vinci began anatomical sketching of the human body
1540	English barbers and surgeons united to form the Barber-Surgeons' Company
1540	Andreas Vesalius discovered that blood flows through the septum in the heart
1543	Vesalius published *De humani corporis fabrica [On the fabric of the human body]*
1570s	Ligatures to stop bleeding and also ointments for wounds developed
1590	The microscope was perfected
1628	William Harvey published his work demonstrating that blood circulates, pumped by the heart
1630	Amputations first performed as a treatment for gangrene
1656	Christopher Wren demonstrated intravenous injection providing the basis for blood transfusion

1658	Dutch naturalist, Jan Swammerdam, observed red blood cells under the microscope
1660s	Thomas Sydenham, a London physician, believed that diagnosis is best done by close observation of symptoms
1665	The plague returned to London
1666	The Great Fire of London
1674	Antonie van Leeuwenhoek, the *Father of Microbiology* described red blood cells
1676	An amateur naturalist discovered bacteria
1701	Giacomo Pylarini, an Italian physician, oversees the first smallpox inoculations
1713	First asylum was established in Norwich – known as Bethel Hospital
1717	Lady Mary Wortley Montagu introduced subcutaneous variolation against smallpox to Britain
1721	Guy's Hospital, London founded
1729	Royal Infirmary, Edinburgh founded
1731	The first recorded appendectomy performed by English surgeon William Cookesley
1739	Queen Charlotte's Maternity Hospital, London founded
1739	First edition published of Samuel Sharp's *A Treatise on the Operations of Surgery*
1753	Dr James Lind published *A treatise of scurvy* following his research in the navy
1796	Edward Jenner developed a vaccination using cowpox to treat smallpox
1799	Humphrey Davy discovered the anaesthetic attributes of nitrous oxide (laughing gas)
1816	The stethoscope was invented by René Laennec in Paris
1818	The first successful blood transfusion to treat post-partum haemorrhage took place
1842	Edwin Chadwick published his *Report on the Sanitary Conditions of the Labouring Population of Great Britain*
1846	First successful use of ether as an anaesthetic in surgery
1847	Prof. James Young Simpson demonstrated chloroform through an experiment on his friends

1846–8	Prevention of the transmission of disease by washing hands before surgery realised
1853	Hypodermic syringe invented independently by both Alexander Wood and Charles Pravaz
1853	The Vaccination Act made smallpox vaccination compulsory from 1 August
1854	Florence Nightingale and Betsi Cadwaladr improved care and hygiene in hospitals at Scutari
1855	Mary Seacole established the *British Hotel* for soldiers near Balaclava
1858	The Medical Act created the General Medical Council to regulate doctors' qualifications
1861	Louis Pasteur published his *Germ Theory*
1865	Elizabeth Garrett-Anderson became the first female doctor in Britain
1867	Joseph Lister began using carbolic acid to dress wounds to fight infection
1870s	Joseph Lister used carbolic acid spray during surgery
1870s	Together Robert Koch and Louis Pasteur established the germ theory of disease
1876	Robert Koch discovered the bacteria that causes anthrax
1887	First contact lenses were developed
1890s	Discovery of antitoxins, and development of vaccines for tetanus and diphtheria
1893	Isolation Hospitals Act enabling local authorities to establish hospitals for infectious diseases
1895	William Röntgen discovered X-rays
1897	Synthesized aspirin developed
1898	Marie Curie discovered the radioactive elements radium and polonium
1901	Blood types first classified into groups
1906	Frederick Gowland Hopkins suggested amino-acids are essential to health
1907	Education (Administrative Provisions) Act requires medical inspections in schools
1908	Old Age Pensions Act (pension commenced 1 January 1909)

1909	Paul Ehrlich pioneers a cure for syphilis and introduces the process known as chemotherapy
1911	National Health Insurance Act became law (came into effect 1 July 1912)
1913	The electro-cardiograph (ECG) introduced for general use by Dr Paul Dudley White
1914	Marie Curie pioneered mobile X-ray facilities on the battlefields of the First World War
1917	Harold Gillies pioneered plastic surgery techniques to repair the faces of injured soldiers
1918	Discovery that trench fever was transmitted by lice
1922	Injected insulin used to treat diabetes for the first time
1928	First true antibiotic, penicillin, discovered by Alexander Fleming
1947	First successful defibrillation performed by Claude Black
1948	Start of the National Health Service in Britain

INTRODUCTION

Two events are an absolute certainty in our lives – birth and death – and this applied to our ancestors too. Throughout their lifetime every one of them could have been ill or injured probably requiring some kind of medical or surgical intervention. They would have suffered from a variety of ailments and diseases, some of which were minor and others of a more serious nature – even life-threatening. Those who served in the military or navy would have been affected by battlefield injuries or illnesses associated with being on board a crowded ship. Families would have been affected by childhood diseases and epidemics which frequently devastated whole communities.

When undertaking family history research, it is important to know the illnesses or diseases that our ancestors suffered which perhaps contributed to or caused their deaths; investigating our ancestors' ailments sheds light on how they coped in their daily lives with their health problems. Conditions common today have often existed for generations and some of these diseases have been inherited from our forebears.

Information about our ancestors' medical history can be found in many official documents like death certificates and hospital or military records, but we should never ignore family letters, wills and obituaries either. We will also need to interpret and understand old medical terms and historic causes of death as well as knowing what caused illness, accident and death throughout the years. Our ancestors could have been involved in accidents at work, particularly after the mechanisation developments of the Industrial Revolution; in those days, health and safety regulations were almost non-existent so accidents were a daily occurrence.

Dedicated medical care was not always available in bygone days and was very dependent on social class. Some of our wealthier ancestors would have benefitted from it while others would not. Some may even have been "on the other side of the fence" working or volunteering in the world of medicine and surgery.

In each historical period, the advances made in medicine were viewed very differently although many treatments, traditions and superstitions overlapped these periods. Advancing medical technologies meant that throughout history, significant improvements were made and some of these are listed in the timeline at the beginning of this book.

Prior to the Victorian era the majority of the population who became ill had to depend on advice from people with no professional medical training; their assistance was actually based upon superstition, astrology or quack remedies. Sick people also relied heavily upon the herbalists and barbers who exhibited skills in early basic surgical procedures.

More wealthy people and those from the upper classes could obtain advice from doctors who, even though "university" qualified, lacked knowledge because there was little if any proven research to back up their theories, diagnoses or treatments. Medicine and its associated disciplines together with funeral etiquette and traditions have truly evolved through time.

From Roman times and the ancient Greeks up to the modern day, there have been many groundbreaking achievements which have formed the basis of ongoing research, ultimately improving treatments and wiping out many diseases and epidemics. The Victorian period was considered to be *the* era of medical advancement – although not always for the better.

CHAPTER 1

EVOLVING MEDICAL INFLUENCES

From medieval times, health and medicine were both very important aspects of our ancestors' lives. Disease and poor health were part of everyday life for our ancestors and medicines were both basic and often useless. Many towns and cities were filthy and knowledge of personal hygiene was frequently non-existent or ignored. In the early periods of history, very few medical professionals neither knew what caused diseases, nor, more importantly, did they know how diseases spread or could be controlled. Most of our early ancestors would have been taught that illness was self-imposed as a result of an individual's behaviour or because of their sins!

Medieval medicine
In the Middle Ages virtually all medical philosophies were influenced by the ancient Greek and Roman philosophy, particularly Galen of Pergamon. Galen was a physician, writer and philosopher who became the most famous doctor in the Roman Empire and whose theories continued to dominate medicine for a further 1,500 years or so. Church leaders looked carefully at Galen's works and decided that, although he was not a Christian, they fitted in with Christian ideals because he referred many times to *the creator* in his works. Physicians believed his ideas were correct and that it was almost impossible to improve on his theories. Therefore translations of Galen's work were accepted as the absolute truth in most medieval medical schools.

Galen believed that the body contained four humours (fluids), namely:

- phlegm
- blood
- yellow bile
- black bile.

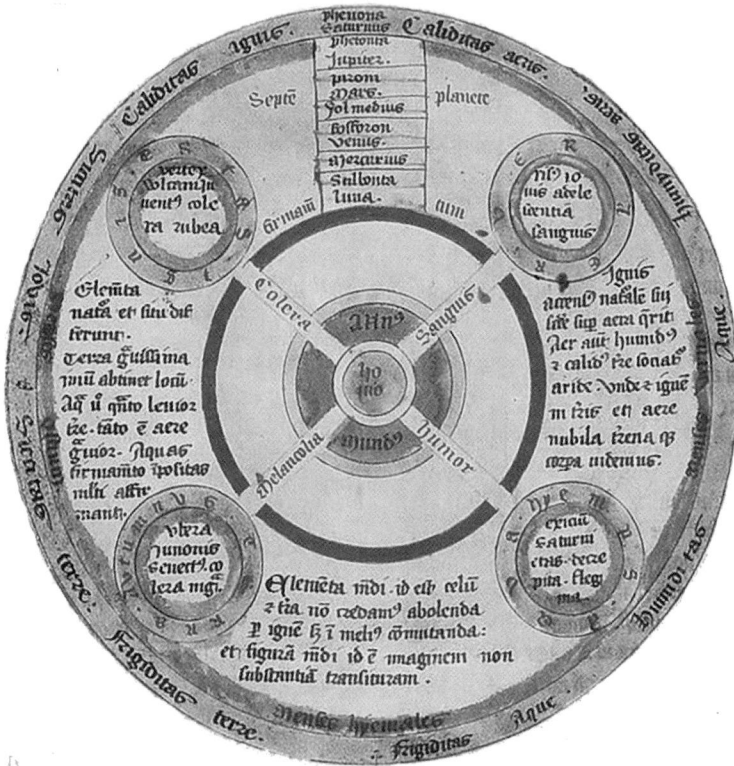

The four humours and how they fit the body and tie in with astrology

If these humours remained in balance then an individual remained healthy; but if an imbalance, occurred they became ill. When illness occurred it was therefore essential to try and keep the balance, which, at the time, was supposedly only achieved by the removal of any excess fluids. The humours theory existed at least until the Renaissance and in many cases for some time thereafter. Alongside this people were also advised to do everything in moderation which helped to keep them balanced and healthy.

Medieval medicine also relied heavily on astrology because it was believed the movement and position of the stars had a significant effect on people's health. The word "influenza" was derived from a medieval word meaning "influence" and was directly attributed to planet alignment. Each part of the body was considered to be associated with an astrological sign and physicians thought medical procedures could only be carried out when the moon was in the correct position; this meant that they needed knowledge of astrology in order to treat their patients effectively. Because doctors believed the stars caused diseases, they consulted reference books containing intricate charts so that they knew exactly when to carry out particular medical procedures. It was also thought that plants and herbs used in medication were under the influence of the planets.

The church also had significant authority because it considered that all illnesses were a punishment for sins and people who became ill were first required to pray fervently to God for forgiveness of their sins. As well as consulting the stars, doctors held many superstitious beliefs, often chanting magical words when treating patients. Many clergymen and doctors also believed that the devil further influenced people's health, so much so that during the late medieval period, the limited medical knowledge handed down from ancient civilisations was frequently replaced by superstition and quackery.

Dissection of dead bodies, including anatomy experiments, was supposedly not allowed and was discouraged by the established Church. Instead they encouraged people to go on crusades to the Holy Land where the Muslim doctors appeared more knowledgeable, and this was said to have given rise to some of the later advances in medical knowledge. Patients even believed that pilgrimages to holy shrines would completely cure them of their illnesses.

During the Renaissance there was a renewed interest shown in the established medical knowledge originating from the ancient Greeks and

Romans. Their medical textbooks were readily available from the mid-1400s because of the advent of the mechanical printing press. Doctors began to experiment and develop new ideas about anatomy and blood circulation resulting in new medical textbooks which began to contain detailed sketches of the human body, thus helping new ideas to spread more rapidly. Renowned artists of the time such as Michelangelo and Leonardo da Vinci studied the human body closely and replicated it in their art works thus helping to increase medical knowledge. The voyages undertaken by Christopher Columbus and Sir Walter Raleigh resulted in the introduction of various herbs and tobacco to England which supported medical treatment and also encouraged people to challenge otherwise established treatments.

In medieval times surgery was rarely undertaken by doctors because various ecclesiastical laws prevented physicians from shedding blood, so it was the barbers or surgeons who conducted their operations outside the recognised medical establishments. Wealthier patients would engage a master surgeon who would complete procedures in the patient's own home. Throughout the Middle Ages, there was an abundant demand for surgery because of continual warfare. However, surgery was held in low regard because many procedures rested with the lesser-trained barber-surgeons. At the time wine was used as an antiseptic although its properties were not fully understood and all surgical treatments remained simple.

Wise women or witches

Lowly manorial tenants and the peasant communities of rural England and Wales usually sought help in times of illness from the parish priest or visited the *wise women* who appeared to exhibit healing skills and occult knowledge. Few people consulted a doctor because they could not afford their fees, so it was normal to be treated by the local wise woman who was skilled in the administration of herbs; the people would also seek spiritual healing by the parish priest or visit the local barber who performed minor surgery and operations and also pulled teeth and set broken bones. These practitioners' cures were a combination of superstition, charms and religion also common for driving evil spirits from mentally ill people. They frequently used herbal remedies, some of which are still in use today in the form of alternative medicines. The sick and dying were often admitted into the monastic hospitals for treatment and care. In many areas the knowledge held by the wise woman had been passed down to her from earlier generations of her family. She also frequently acted as the midwife delivering babies. Her skills were highly valued particularly amongst womenfolk.

Even today herbs are grown for medicinal purposes. Herb garden at Syon Abbey.

In the early Middle Ages people accepted both magic and witchcraft as part of life but by the fourteenth century a philosophy existed that witches were servants of the devil. Many wise women were also deemed to be witches and some were unjustly tried, found guilty of witchcraft and subsequently put to death. The Witchcraft Act of 1563 introduced the death penalty for any sorcery used to cause someone's death. Therefore, witchcraft became a capital offence in Britain in 1563 but since 1484 the Pope had also deemed it to be heresy. Most rumoured witches were female – poor, elderly and often widowed. Many unfortunate women were condemned and then hanged after undergoing appalling torture. The use of thumbscrews and *caspie-claws*, a type of leg iron which was heated over a brazier before being applied, usually resulted in an unfounded confession of guilt from those accused even though most did not practise witchcraft. Matthew Hopkins, an unsuccessful lawyer, became known as the *Witchfinder General*, assuming the role as late as 1644–45. There were various other sentences pronounced on witches. They may have been given *the swimming test* where her thumbs were tied to opposite big toes after which she was thrown into the river or lake. If she floated she was guilty and subsequently sentenced to death: if she sank she was innocent but subjected to an *unfortunate accident*.

So, was your ancestor classed as a witch?

There were many witch trials held throughout the sixteenth and early seventeenth centuries.

Some of the most prominent were trials at:

- Warboys, Cambridgeshire 1589–1593 – these trials were instrumental in the passing of the 1604 Witchcraft Act
- North Berwick, Scotland 1590–1592 – gave rise to around 3,500 witches being executed in Scotland
- Pendle, Lancashire 1612–1634
- Belvoir, Leicestershire 1618–1619
- Bury St Edmunds, Suffolk 1645–1694
- Bideford, Devon 1682.

Witch trials in England happened between the early fifteenth and the end of the seventeenth centuries. There were approximately 1000 people tried, of which ninety per cent were women. Most of the trials took place during the Civil War and the Puritan period.

Many innocent wise women were amongst those subjected to execution. The Reformation made little difference as both Catholics and Protestants continued to hold the same view about witchcraft. Women were accused of using their powers to cause impotence or disease, stillborn infants and turning milk sour. Execution by burning at the stake was the main punishment for those found guilty. Records, where they survive, can be found in early assize records alongside some appeals to higher courts including some in the Court of Arches.

Tudor medicine

The Tudor period 1485–1558 was a time when only about one in ten people lived beyond their forties and medical practices stagnated. Bleeding (or bloodletting) continued to be generally accepted as the most practical cure for most illnesses because people continued to believe that too much blood was bad for the body. The philosophy behind that belief was that if blood was released (or let) from the body, then illnesses would subside. Some medical practitioners used leeches for the procedure, a practice which is becoming popular again today, but many practitioners just cut into a vein and let the blood flow.

Herbal remedies predominated widely and were the recognised treatment for most of the common ailments. For relief from headaches a mixture of sage, lavender and marjoram was used and chamomile was taken to reduce stomach ache. Tudors referred to herbal remedies as 'simples' and most women would know how to make them. Virtually all Tudor medical cures were based on earlier established remedies, particularly for the control of smallpox and jaundice which were common occurrences amongst the population.

The Tudor era also saw the introduction of specialist doctors; the type of doctor consulted depended upon how wealthy patients were and also where they lived. Wealthy people received home visits from physicians or surgeons but the barbers continued to extract rotten teeth and carry out bloodletting. Apothecaries of the day sold medicines and herbal remedies. Medieval medical practices prevailed, particularly within the poorer communities who would continue to receive basic health care from their own family, from the church or by visiting the local wise woman.

Specialist plague doctors treated those suffering from diseases such as bubonic plague and other infections such as typhoid. To do so, doctors would dress top to toe in vinegar-doused protective clothing and wear a "beak-like" mask, boots and gloves. They often examined a patient's urine checking its smell, colour and even taste! Astrology continued as the key element in diagnosis.

The plague doctor dressed in PPE of the day

Tudor doctors actively helped advance medical knowledge basing their findings on actual observation and evidence, helped by the drawings of the human anatomy, rather than relying on traditions and superstitions as in the past. During the Renaissance period, there was an increase in experimental medical investigations, particularly in the dissection of the body which paved the way for advancing knowledge of human anatomy.

Many of the illnesses and diseases that existed in Tudor times remained untreated or misdiagnosed; this was due to a lack of understanding of basic hygiene and the effects of the filthy living conditions still endured by most people as well as medical ignorance. Tudor medicine remained very basic and inadequate for dealing with the diseases of the day.

The advancement of neurology began as early as the sixteenth century and was deemed to be the start of a deeper understanding of medical sciences thus enabling doctors to improve their diagnoses, but this had little effect on health care for some time. Opium, quinine, various folklore cures and the use of poisonous metal-based compounds were popular but misused treatments often led to serious and perhaps unknown consequences.

Tudor home-grown medicine

When Tudor folk felt unwell, in the first instance they resorted to the household medicine cabinet stocked with treatments made from garden produce. Virtually every cottage had a garden planted with food crops and a large variety of herbs, many of which were grown only for medicinal purposes and for fabric dyeing. The more common herbs were winter savory used in herbal cordials for gastric complaints and was said to be a good remedy for colic; lemon balm to ease anxiety, aid restful sleep, alleviate skin problems and repel irritating insects and fennel to quieten hiccups, ease nausea, aid digestion and soothe coughs and eye infections.

When people succumbed to more serious illnesses, there was generally a *herb wife*, the successor to the wise woman, living on the edge of the village or close by who would have more land on which to grow an abundance of medicinal herbs as well as being able to forage for many from the wild close to her cottage. Again her skill and knowledge would have been passed down the generations. In most instances she was paid in kind for her services, usually with commodities such as eggs, meat or something useful for her and affordable to the patient. Tudor girls were taught by their mothers how to manage the garden and because many herbs didn't grow in winter, they would have been gathered and dried so they were available throughout the year.

Stuart medicine

Stuart medicine saw several advances but doctors' knowledge was still very rudimentary. By the middle of the seventeenth century, there were signs emerging of a greater understanding of diseases and cures but this all came to a devastating halt due to the 1665 plague which hit the country. The 1665 plague was the worst outbreak of disease in England since the Black Death in the mid 1300s, notwithstanding that other sporadic but often minor outbreaks of bubonic plague had occurred throughout the medieval and Tudor periods.

Some of the cures used in the treatment of the 1665 plague were rudimentary and indeed the only ones that the poor would have been able to use. It was believed that fragrant smells would drive the plague away so many people carried highly-scented flowers around with them. Although thought to have pagan origins, or even be associated with the Black Death, modern belief claims that the nursery rhyme *Ring-a-ring-o'-roses* is about the 1665 plague. Roses represent the red blotches on the skin; posies relate to the fragrant flowers carried by people to ward off the plague and *atishoo* relates to the sneezing fits experienced by those suffering from the plague. *We all fall down* clearly refers to people dying, usually suddenly.

To counteract the effects of the plague, people just stayed indoors and some even relocated to rural areas from the towns and cities. Doctors advised fumigation of houses and keeping the windows closed. People kept their distance from each other and money was dropped into jars of vinegar. Other people carried bottles of perfume and wore lucky charms.

Several quack cures existed at this time which shows how superstitions affected medical knowledge. Some physicians took these to extremes by wearing a dead toad around their neck; they considered that doing so would ward off the plague as they went about treating their patients. Other superstitious cures included carrying a lucky hare's foot, dried toad, leeches, the letters *abracadabra* written in a triangle and pressing a plucked chicken against the sores until it died. Others believed that smoke cured the plague and advised people to burn anything that would create smoke; many burnt cowhides. Some physicians believed that making the victims sweat would also cure them.

Around three-quarters of a million people died nationwide from the Great Plague in 1665. The Great Fire of London the following year in 1666 is thought to have gone a long way to ridding the area of the plague which was essentially centred on the City of London.

A medical renaissance – the pattern of change 1500-1700
The medical advances over this two-hundred-year period can be likened to a signpost at a T-junction – one direction pointing backwards to the Middle

Ages and the other pointing forwards … albeit with little directional information because medical professionals were unaware of what lay ahead.

By the 1700s traditions still prevailed but changes began to occur albeit very slowly. The treatment and prevention of illness did not change much because the traditional herbal remedies appeared to work; the other reason nothing much happened was because the causes of disease were still not fully understood. Up to this time treatment and prevention were still linked to unproven ideas about the causes of disease. People's lives were still very much dominated by religion – many believed that God had a major involvement in them becoming ill. People were also convinced that bad air was a common explanation for catching a disease; overcrowded towns caused pungent smells which made the air appear 'bad'. This bad air theory persisted well into the Victorian period.

Physicians continued to accept the theory of the four humours and so continued with the conventional balancing treatments. People were encouraged to continue to pray and use herbal remedies that they knew from experience helped recovery. Some new remedies were introduced such as tobacco, which actually did more harm than good, and quinine which proved to help cure various fevers.

Georgian and Regency medicine

In the eighteenth and early nineteenth centuries, existing medical beliefs were socially very clear and institutionally identified. Earlier traditional medicinal cures also survived at this time, the common treatments being leeches, medical soaps, white wine and vinegar.

Leeches were used to bleed patients suffering from cornea problems and were applied on a patient's arms when irritation was apparent or to reduce glandular swelling. Medical soaps were recommended for patients who suffered from syphilis or herpes and the cure for reducing a swelling thyroid gland was to drink white wine and wear a bag of ammonia around your neck!

The first time the country experienced massive population growth was in the Georgian period; one of the main reasons for this was the forward-looking developments in medical sciences which helped improve life expectancy. Various epidemics in Britain caused lower population numbers because of high death rates. Plagues and smallpox were both fatal and as a result many infants and children were dying before they reached two or three years of age. However, by the start of the Georgian era, plagues were almost a thing of the past and a possible vaccination against smallpox had been discovered, but was not widely practised.

During the eighteenth century food was reasonably plentiful because agricultural advancements meant that the country was able to produce sufficient food to feed the increasing population. Medical practices also improved although surgery was still at an early stage and many physicians still used old and established methods of care.

The medical profession still had little knowledge about the transfer of germs; it was very common for households to throw their waste into streets. Cleanliness, or the lack of it, was an issue in most workplaces as people were employed in establishments where the environment posed major health risks associated with poor working conditions. Children began work from the age of six or seven resulting in them being exposed to a number of respiratory diseases; adults suffered from innumerable health risks in the workplace too and increased mechanisation led to many fatalities due to industrial accidents.

Upper-class people suffered health problems because of overeating and obesity. Dental problems, heart diseases and diabetes were very common among these classes. Horse-riding became popular, both as a sport and for leisure, but accidents often happened in which many lost their limbs or even died.

The medical problems associated with alcohol affected all social classes. Alcoholic drinks made from corn were produced on a large scale so these drinks were affordable for poor and rich alike. Known as *mother gin*, its availability resulted in many more alcoholics as well as posing other health-related threats and deaths from sclerosis of the liver and serious mental disorders.

Many people continued to live in unhealthy social surroundings as there was still little awareness of personal hygiene across all classes. For the poor people, the supply of water was limited so it was used for cooking and other essential purposes first rather than using for personal hygiene. While the rich were conscious about how they looked, personal cleanliness was not a priority. Most people only bathed once a week – it almost became a ritual – because water had to be carried to the portable bath. Piped water was only available in a laundry which was usually detached from the houses. Public bathing was frowned upon. However, the upper classes kept themselves presentable by using perfumes and fragrances to suppress their body odour, hiding behind thick makeup and regularly changing their clothes; this was a practice limited to the social classes that could afford to do it. The poor continued to live with unsanitary conditions and as such were still prone to many airborne and waterborne diseases. As well as infant deaths, mothers often died during or just after childbirth. Although food was plentiful there was little, if any, awareness of its nutritional values although people usually made up for any deficient nutrients through their routine diets.

The advent of quack medicine

Quackery can be defined loosely as health fraud and those who practised it, the quacks, abounded in the eighteenth century. Commercial medicine was plentiful at this time and was traded on earlier established values of religious healing. Quacks did not want to disrupt the foundations of the medical strongholds like the colleges, but they tried their hardest to wheedle their way into them. Many quacks were hugely successful, climbing the social ladder and aspiring to recognition which meant some even received honours or titles. To become socially accepted was very important to them and was often achieved by mixing their claims with religious motives. Many travelling missionaries were also peddlers in quack medicines.

The many socio-economic opportunities of the eighteenth century shaped all realms of medical practice. The educated physicians and surgeons had channels of advancement at their disposal including the important patronage networks amongst upper-class society. Many quacks sustained their medical livelihood by taking chances and opportunities primarily because of the development of the big business of selling medical goods.

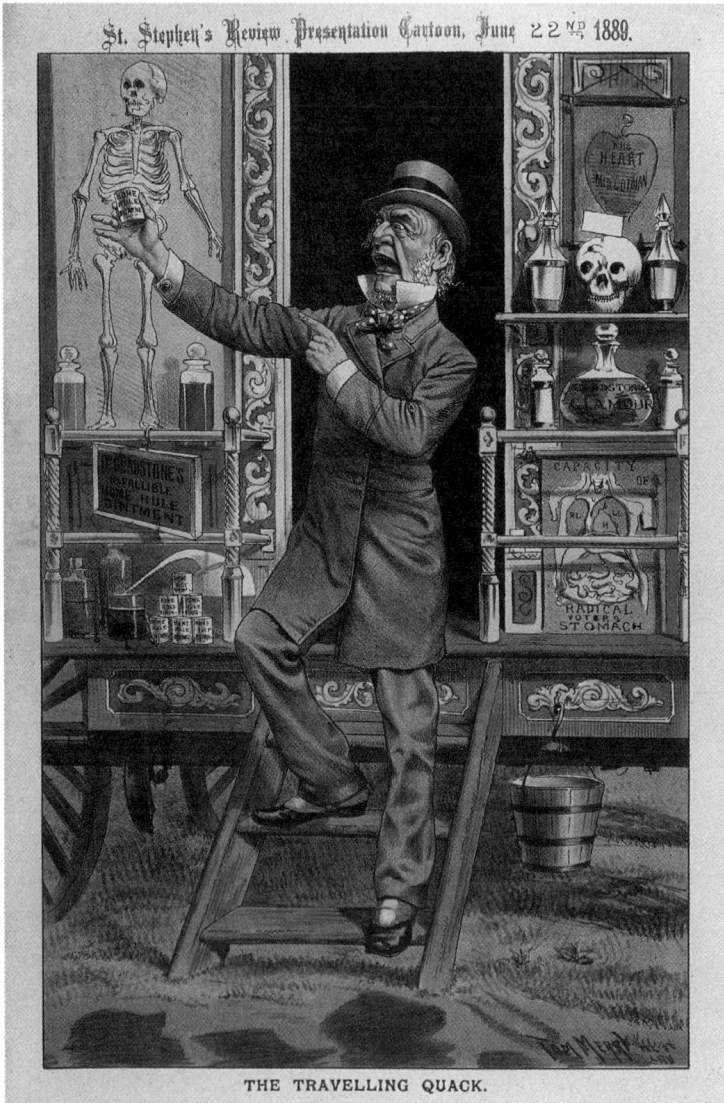

Typical travelling quack doctor selling medicines from a caravan

There were perhaps five main reasons for the success of quacks in the eighteenth century:

- low therapeutic effectiveness of Georgian medicine
- writings of contemporary doctors
- Bills of Mortality showing just how inadequately medicine coped with disease and illness
- extent of gastro-enteric diseases in infancy
- increase in tuberculosis.

Bills of Mortality were weekly statistics which monitored burials, initially in London from 1592 to 1595 and then more or less continuously between 1603 and 1840. After 1611 the responsibility for producing the statistics was assigned to the Worshipful Company of Parish Clerks. The geographic area covered by the bills expanded as London grew. New parishes were added at the time when the ancient parishes were divided. However, the number of bills declined from the 1820s because parishes became haphazard in providing returns and ultimately the bills were superseded in 1840 by the returns made to the registrar general.

When diseases prevailed and medical treatments were unreliable, people resorted to cures including traditional folk potions, proprietary medicines and quack remedies. The colleges of physicians and surgeons were legally empowered to restrict their own memberships. From the seventeenth century, the College of Physicians actively enforced its rights to prosecute intruders. Notwithstanding this, medical practices in Georgian times had virtually no restrictions. There was no medical register, no licensing system and no penalties for irregular practice. In London admission to both the colleges continued to be restricted and yet, much to their annoyance, the opportunistic quacks enjoyed official approval. It was not unusual for foreign quacks to obtain royal licences to practise in England and many quacks took out legal patents for their remedies – and this continued into the early Victorian era

All this was possible because within the medical world at that time, patient power predominated. Even in the medieval era doctors were obliged to their patient for specifying symptoms and to some degree their treatment. It was an age where the commercial and business sides of medicine were inseparable because of the evolving consumer society; this was helped by the fact that the middle classes now had surplus income and they were eager to spend it.

There are several aspects of quackery which are worth emphasising.

- Quacks exploited new market opportunities, especially in directing their appeal to the affluent classes. In Tudor and Stuart times, the quack was an individual who operated in the marketplace but during the mid-eighteenth century upmarket quacks emerged who were also skilled showmen.
- Quack medicine evolved from personal service to the permanent medical commodity. The sixteenth- and seventeenth-century quack concocted and sold his own medicines but the focus shifted from the person to the power of the medicine itself. This resulted in such products as *Dr James' Powders*, *Hooper's Female Pills* and *Stoughton's Great Cordial Elixir* some of which were advertised as *approved by eminent physicians of the college*. The advertising campaigns saturated the marketplace thus these medicines became extremely popular.
- These 'advertising physicians' showed daring both in marketing and packaging frequently resorting to gimmicks. This process came to the fore after the Restoration, initially as a result of circulating handbills, advertising in the coffee houses and later by using wall posters.
- Newspapers and periodicals of the time were vital to marketing the remedies both from a publicity and outlet perspective. Some newspaper offices even acted as depots for the sale of the proprietary medicines and newspaper boys often delivered a parcel of medicine at the same time as the morning paper. The links between quacks and the newspaper publishing industry were intertwined throughout most of the Georgian and Regency periods.

Self-medication in Georgian times
There were no effective controls over medical practices at a time when the royal medical colleges continually failed in their endeavours to enforce

a closed shop for the benefit of their members, which firmly suggested financial rather than medical benefits. In most rural areas, irrespective of social class, who was considered as a doctor was dependent on who was available and thus it was irrelevant whether they were professionally qualified or not. Country physicians' earnings were always significantly less than their urban counterparts and in some locations there was no access to any medical professional at all so self-medication was often the only alternative.

Some of the more well-known self-medication cures included:

- *Essence of Water Dock* – a common cure for scurvy, leprosy, and many other disorders
- *Tincture of Centaury* – supposedly a good stomachic cordial and stimulating medicine providing a healthy appetite and sound digestion by strengthening weak stomachs
- *Pectoral Honey* – supposedly an immediate cure for coughs, colds, and consumption
- Established herb remedies practised in the earlier periods of history were also commonplace.

Virtually everyone practised self-medication particularly in the 1700s; household books of the day contained various recipes to treat common illnesses. Prominent and influential members of the community including John Wesley, the founder of Methodism, and Horace Walpole were committed to self-medication.

Many early provincial newspapers carried medical advice. Many households also had a *home-doctor* book, perhaps the most well-known being *Domestic Medicine* written by William Buchan, a Scottish physician and author. The book contained warnings against using various quack and folk remedies.

The Georgian attitude to medicine seemed to be that the common outcome of medical treatment was failure, so it was considered the responsibility of the person suffering the sickness or their family to exercise self-control and many kept trying alternatives until one worked – or the affected person died. Professional doctors were generally well-respected within the communities in which they practised but their diagnosis and treatment was not always accepted.

Regency influences

The period between 1811 and 1820 was known as the Regency era; this when George, Prince George of Wales ruled while his father, George III, was deemed incapable of ruling because of his madness. This period covered a time of great social, political, and economic change; medically speaking, war with Napoleon enabled the medical profession to gain more knowledge and improve treatments.

Society became even more class-conscious than previously. In the less affluent areas of England and Wales, stealing, womanising, gambling and constant alcohol consumption was widespread and there was also a small population boom. Marriage was rarely as a result of romance. It was a male-dominated world; when a woman married, control of her passed from that of her father to that of her husband. Remaining single was seen as a misfortune and was not really a viable option for women of any class.

The age of consent was twelve years for girls and fourteen years for boys and remained so until 1929, but parental consent to marry by licence was needed for minors under the age of twenty-one. Most couples did not marry until they were in their early to mid-twenties or even later, particularly if the groom was serving an apprenticeship. Many apprentices were bound for seven years from the age of fourteen and were forbidden to marry during that time. Sex before marriage was not illegal, although under the Bastardy Acts, unmarried pregnant women were compelled to name the father or could be forced to marry if they fell on hard times and approached the authorities for any form of relief.

Hardwicke's Marriage Act of 1753 stipulated that marriage banns should be read on three Sundays in the parish church of residence of both parties. Besides announcing the impending marriage to the congregation, it was an open invitation for parental objections or others and it was particularly relevant in cases of minors wanting to marry. As many family historians will encounter only one set of marriage banns, the system meant that residency was given as the same address or location for both parties which avoided payment of double banns fees with the parties only paying for one set of banns.

Throughout history generally, the main objective of marriage was to have children. Upper-class men needed male heirs to continue the family name and fortune, while working-class couples wanted children to contribute towards the family income and to help support them later in life. Too many children became a burden but it was difficult to limit the number of times a woman became pregnant because reliable contraceptives were unknown. Condoms were used mainly by prostitutes to avoid sexually-transmitted disease rather than for contraception. Large families were considered a good idea because there was a greater chance of some children being spared during epidemics and surviving beyond infancy.

Victorian medicine 1837–1901

The social structure of the Victorians influenced the way all classes viewed the medical remedies available to them. The population growth in the nineteenth century meant most families remained large although many suffered high infant mortality as well as unhealthy working and living conditions. Many women encountered complications because of multiple pregnancies and childbirth continued to have fatal consequences for some mothers.

The upper classes suffered as a result of overeating and sporting accidents together with many alcohol-related issues, whilst the poorer classes suffered because of slums, overcrowding and public health issues. Most people were reasonably active and the increased availability of fresh fruit helped everyone work towards a healthier lifestyle.

Medical advances and improved methods of surgery allowed doctors to spend more time examining patients although newer medicines developed to treat many ailments often caused additional problems and side effects which had not been encountered or even envisaged. The medical schools gave more medical students, surgeons and doctors greater opportunities to learn and enhance their skills.

By the turn of the twentieth century medical discoveries had allowed patients to access effective diagnostic procedures and benefit from the new technologies. Advances in public health, science and regulation within the professions also contributed to this new professionalism. Surgery had undergone massive change and doctors started wearing white coats and stethoscopes were carried as a basic diagnostic instrument.

In many areas of the country death rates from diseases and surgery began to decrease albeit only slightly. For every disease that was in decline, such as cholera and smallpox, other diseases significantly increased. Many urban areas still experienced overcrowding and appalling living conditions. Large numbers of those who volunteered for military service in the later Victorian wars and the First World War were prevented from serving because they were deemed unfit on medical grounds. Throughout the Victorian era the medical profession made great advances but by modern standards some of the cures and medicines available, either prescribed or over the counter, would be discounted today as dangerous.

Most family historians will be fully aware of the perceived relatively short life expectancy of our Victorian ancestors. People born in England and Wales in the late eighteenth to mid-nineteenth centuries would probably have lost both their parents before they reached adulthood. Infant mortality in England and Wales peaked around the 1890s. However, many people survived into their eighties and nineties.

It is also thought that the urban diet in mid-Victorian times provided protection against major degenerative diseases and that life expectancy continued to improve during the latter half of the nineteenth century. Some of the health benefits of an improved diet were lost because of the increasing use of preservative chemicals in mass-produced and refined foods. Nevertheless, improved nutrition in England and Wales was most important in the reduction of early deaths. Better sanitation also played a part in reducing the number of deaths from gastro-intestinal infections and improved nutrition also resulted in a lower death rate from tuberculosis. All circumstances depended upon social class, lifestyle, living conditions and diet.

Effects of the Industrial Revolution on lifestyle

In the aftermath of the Industrial Revolution, mid-nineteenth century Britain became the world's premier manufacturing powerhouse although it was still a predominantly rural-based society. Irrespective of whether families lived in industrialised urban areas or in agricultural rural areas, the majority of the population were from the poorer classes. In urban areas, labourers worked in heavy industry, on construction or in mining. They also provided a massive force of domestic servants. In the large urban industrial regions more than half the population had migrated from rural districts.

Agricultural labourers were by far the largest sector among the poor labouring people. By the mid-nineteenth century, land enclosure was mostly complete and farming was predominantly commercial in England, Wales and the Lowlands of Scotland. This also meant that the labourers' work was frequently seasonal, intermittent or seriously affected by the agricultural depressions. Local economics fuelled the migration to urban areas where jobs were more plentiful, meaning more regular employment and generally higher wages, usually offset by poorer living conditions and higher commodity costs. Agricultural regions were also affected by their own cultural, economies and living conditions.

Generally there were appalling sanitary conditions in urban areas, but by the same token, living conditions were not idyllic in rural communities either. Housing was often poor, overcrowded or squalid. Water supplies, mainly from wells, were often limited and other means of domestic water supplies were often contaminated. Polluted water was common in low-lying countryside, particularly marshlands or along river estuaries. The situation gradually improved as the twentieth century approached.

In many areas of the country white bread was the staple part of the diet for many in the poorer classes, sometimes supplemented by vegetables, fruit, meat, fish and dairy products. Although the price of bread fell after the repeal of the Corn Laws in 1846, poor urban families had limited resources to purchase produce that gave them an adequate balanced diet. Many poor urban families lived on bread and potatoes with little or no meat or milk and in some families they drank tea with sugar but no milk. This diet was much the same for poor rural agricultural workers. Many rural families also subsisted on bread with little milk or meat. Fish did not figure in rural areas unless they were located within coastal areas. It may seem surprising that milk was not easily obtainable in the countryside but farmers produced it commercially for sale to the urban wealthier families so local supplies were hard to come by. However, the rural diet was sometimes better in some areas of England because of *payments made in kind*. Employers or landowners would often pay part of a wage in items such as grain, potatoes, meat, milk or the provision of a small allotment enabling families to grow their own potatoes and vegetables or perhaps rear a pig or chickens.

CHAPTER TWO

THE CIVILIAN MEDICAL PROFESSION

Those practising medicine in whatever capacity would have been essential to most of our ancestors' lives irrespective of when and how they lived. It is probable that somewhere in your family tree you will find an ancestor who followed one of the diverse medical occupations either as civilians, within the military or in a volunteer role.

Your ancestor may have been a doctor, surgeon, nurse, midwife, apothecary, dentist, a specialist in an area of medicine or even a quack. They may have been involved with voluntary charities and endowed hospitals – particularly in the sixteenth to eighteenth centuries. Some would have been deployed to the battlefields as stretcher-bearers or orderlies in times of war. Many would have become involved with the voluntary organisations such as the Red Cross or Voluntary Aid Detachments. All of them would have played a vital role in the work which, as we have already seen, evolved over time and would have an effect on all our families.

In the earlier periods of history the physicians held more prestige but were not concerned or interested in surgical procedures; one of their prime roles was prescribing drugs to the patients that consulted them. In Victorian times in order to practise as a physician, a licence from Royal College of Physicians was a mandatory requirement.

Surgeons were considered subordinate particularly within the Georgian and Victorian medical hierarchy but they did most things that a physician wouldn't do. Initially surgeons were not as well-respected in the community as physicians, possibly because of their established connection with barbers. The difference in status was also reflected in the way they were addresses as Mr. as opposed to Dr.

Apothecaries were considered to be the lower sector within the medical hierarchy. They initially issued the medicines prescribed by the physicians but also advised patients on medical matters, a forerunner role to that of a pharmacist.

There was much medical advancement during the Victorian era; many of the changes were so positive that illnesses began to be perceived differently by the public and that brought about many changes in the treatment and diagnosis of diseases.

Medieval doctors and dentists

Medieval physicians generally only treated wealthy patients. Some doctors received their medical qualifications through the monasteries or from the early medical schools or universities, and some even studied at foreign universities. Through the medical education facilities, they learnt about Arabic and ancient Greek medicine, the foundation of modern practice.

Doctors, however, were not always trusted among their rich patients. The medieval doctors and barber-surgeons gained much of their experience treating wounds and broken bones because of injuries sustained during the many wars of the period. They pioneered setting broken bones in plaster and also how to seal wounds with egg whites to prevent infection. They used alcohol or certain plants as crude anaesthetics to try and dull the pain during operations. They were also the first to practise caesarean section to deliver babies.

There were a few dentists in the Middle Ages in Britain and they were used mostly by the wealthier classes. Dentists were able to remove decay, carry out fillings, strengthen loose teeth with metal wires and fit false teeth which were generally made from the bones of an ox. The lower classes would visit the barber-surgeon for basic dental treatment.

Very few people reached old age and if they did, they were not always in the best of health because many suffered from infections, broken bones or developed chronic illnesses. From the thirteenth century many doctors gained their experience by being apprenticed to established practitioners. Apothecaries began to supply medicines made from plant, mineral and animal substances. Some practitioners were only employed to cater for medical emergencies on the battlefields.

Most medieval doctors operated in a predominantly Christian society and full recovery from illness was seen to be dependent on the patient's religious devotion. A church council in 1215 instructed people to first seek the support of a priest because sickness of the body was considered to be the result of sin, so parish priests, monks and nuns all played an important role in treating the sick.

Physicians coped with the diseases and illnesses of the time which were not just physical and mental disorders but also those caused by spiritual complaints. Doctors therefore battled daily with witchcraft, astrology and other astronomical events as well as mortal enemies. An astrological evaluation was an important part of any physician's diagnosis but practitioners also evaluated diet and the amount of physical exercise undertaken. Hippocratic doctors were fairly advanced in the knowledge of anatomy and surgery but had very little medical knowledge. Monasteries, established by various Christian religions, also became the centres of study. Monks grew plants, distilled liquors and copied and translated ancient medical textbooks so they became pioneers of the day in both medicine and health.

Medieval surgery

Galen was a skilled surgeon perhaps best known for developing a surgical procedure for the removal of cataracts, the basics of which are still in use today. Surgery was developing, centred on the practices of individual methods rather than standardized procedures.

The early medical schools began to develop a uniform study of surgery in the late twelfth century when formal teaching of surgical techniques began. Surgeons who were travelling with the armies during the crusades were tasked with declaring whether a casualty was dead or not. Surgeons considered themselves to be "elite" and were distinct from the barbers who performed tasks which the surgeons considered too mundane for them to perform. Barber-surgeons were far more common than trained surgeons but they were regulated and only allowed to carry out certain treatments. Trained surgeons were also limited because surgery was deemed to be high-risk and often a last resort. Surgery inevitably resulted in infections such as gangrene which usually proved fatal. Forward-thinking surgeons often treated wounds with brine. Using alcohol to clean a wound was a much later development despite being widely used as a painkiller.

Burns were common, given the open-hearth fires and the use of naked flames as a source of light. Flaming arrows fired by archers, bundles of burning faggots tossed by catapults, boiling water and oil were the standard weapons of war. Burns received from boiling pots and cauldrons were also very common in the home. Doctors treated burns by concentrating on preventing the injured area from becoming dry; nevertheless, severe burns were usually fatal. Doctors did all they could to prevent burns from blistering by applying ointments. The ointment was applied and reapplied as necessary to prevent the burn area from drying out. This form of successful treatment was attributed mainly to experiences gained by surgeons on the battlefield.

Injured limbs, whether as a result of war or from domestic accidents, were usually amputated – hopefully to ensure the patient's survival. Simple fractures could be set and allowed to heal over time with the support of splints or casts but compound fractures could not be set so amputation was the only alternative. Medieval surgeons developed casts for broken limbs made from a flour and egg mixture which, when hardened, could keep a broken limb in place provided it was not weight-bearing. Battlefield surgeons considered speed to be an important factor in successful amputations in order to reduce shock. Proficient surgeons could amputate a limb in less than a minute but then spent time afterwards controlling the bleeding by means of cauterization or using ligatures on blood vessels.

Tudor doctors

Tudor doctors were largely ignorant of the dangers of the open sewers which ran through towns and cities; this was further aggravated by pollution and the diseases emanating from rubbish being dumped in the streets and water courses. Tudor houses were built very close together in narrow streets so common illnesses and diseases were very easily transmitted. Doctors did not acknowledge that many diseases of the time were spread by the lice, fleas and vermin which existed not only in the streets but also in houses. Medical advances in the fifteenth and sixteenth centuries were almost non-existent and practices of the medieval era still prevailed.

Doctors frequently wore a face mask so they did not inhale germs from airborne diseases. Masks had a *beak* on the front of them and the end of the beak was a reservoir for oils or herbs which masked smells. Bizarrely, because of their superstitious nature and lack of understanding of the various diseases, they would also wear an amulet of ground-up toad and dried blood around their waists for protection. Their boots, thick gloves and long clothes also protected them from infections from flea bites.

Georgian and Regency medical practitioners

There was a distinct hierarchy in the Georgian medical world, semi-established by the Tudors. The College of Physicians was mainly for university-educated physicians; the Incorporation of Surgeons was for surgeons who were apprenticed and the Apothecaries' Company was obviously for apothecaries. Georgian society also had various other practitioners including the wise-women, midwives, nurses, chemists, grocers and the itinerant quack pedlars.

'Quack' became a derogatory term used by the physicians who considered those people as incompetent fraudsters or cheats. The dictionary defines a quack as *a boastful pretender to arts which he does not understand, a vain boastful pretender to physic, one who proclaims his own medical abilities in public places or an artful, tricking practitioner in physic.*

There were several kinds of medical practitioners in the eighteenth and nineteenth centuries.

Physicians

Physicians generally remained at the top of the social ladder within their profession and were considered "gentlemen". They continued to simply diagnose patients and write prescriptions. Many were in the same social circle as the families they treated, often dining with them or being a weekend guest.

Surgeons

Surgeons learned their trade in a hands-on situation with an experienced older surgeon. They did not always perform surgery but many practised in general medicine in much the same style as a modern GP.

Apothecaries

Apothecaries also learned their trade by serving an apprenticeship. They were ranked further down the hierarchy than their counterparts. As a group they separated from the Worshipful Company of Grocers and became a new livery company, The Worshipful Society of Apothecaries, established in 1617. Their primary role was to dispense the prescriptions written by the physicians. However, in many rural areas apothecaries also functioned as surgeons and gave general medical advice.

Midwives and accouchers

Mortality rates as a result of childbirth were high and fever was a significant risk because of the lack of sound hygiene practices around childbirth. Higher survival rates were achieved by using the services of a midwife who largely gained their experience in hands-on situations. In the late Georgian and Regency era, *accoucheurs*, who were mainly men, specialized in the whole process of childbirth from conception to delivery – basically what we would call a male midwife.

Barbers / Dentists

Until 1859 there was no formal education or qualification for those providing dental treatment. It wasn't until after the First World War when dentists had to be qualified to practise. So prior to that, barbers usually performed dental procedures but limited their practice to extracting or filling teeth.

Victorian professionals

Before the General Medical Council was formed there were around twenty different bodies involved in regulating the medical profession in Britain. Each body or organisation used different criteria to assess a person's medical knowledge and test their competence. At the start of the Victorian era about one third of all doctors were still unqualified. A doctor practising in one area would generally not be able to do so in another, so there was no uniform scheme of listing those qualified to practise medicine throughout Britain.

Medical regulation

Regulation was introduced to make sure that medicine was only practised by qualified people. Regulating medical practice actually commenced as early as 1421 when Parliament was petitioned with the request that nobody be allowed to practise medicine without qualifications. The earliest regulation and thus licensing was under the auspices of the church although the established universities also had a significant role.

However, in the 1500s medical practice in England was not regulated resulting in a high proportion of patients suffering fatalities during treatment. The leading physicians of the early sixteenth century wanted the power to grant licences only to those with qualifications and to punish unqualified practitioners and any person engaging in malpractice.

Despite acceptance in Parliament, little happened until 1511 when regulation of the medical profession was granted to the bishops. The 1511 statute began a process to eliminate unqualified practitioners. The 1511 Act required both physicians and surgeons to be licensed by the church diocese covering the area in which they practised. At the time this was the most widespread system of "qualification" throughout England and Wales. Although the Act was not repealed until 1948, it had fallen into disuse by about 1750 and it is unlikely that ecclesiastical licences will be found much after that date. The criteria for obtaining a licence included both medical experience and good character.

Seven years later the College of Physicians was established and they assumed responsibility for licensing doctors, but only in London. In 1523 an Act of Parliament extended its powers to include all of England and Wales. Various disputes subsequently arose between the colleges, universities, and bishops over licensing. Depending upon the practice areas, the doctors' diocesan boundaries could often be crossed so licences were needed from different bishops; thus the two archbishops (Canterbury and York) were authorised to issue provincial licences in such circumstance. By the early 1600s around a quarter of doctors had received their licences from archbishops.

The *Lancet* founded in 1823 and the British Medical Association founded in 1832 promoted medical discoveries and helped to maintain the integrity of the medical profession. The publication of the *British Medical Journal* in 1853 preceded the Medical Act of 1858. The General Medical Council published an annual register of those with specified qualifications who were entitled to practise. Those who had been practising since 1815 or before were allowed to be included. Any person not appearing in the register but practising was liable to censure and a heavy penalty.

The General Medical Council took overall responsibility for medical education in 1858 and was originally established as the General Council of Medical Education and Registration of the United Kingdom. Besides their responsibility for registration and medical education, they also published the *Pharmacopoeia* which listed all available drugs and gave instructions about their usage. Compiling the first medical register was a complex process so its publication was delayed beyond the original target date. Of those who applied to be included in the register, some doctors were subsequently removed from the 1860 register because they remained unqualified.

Medical education
Rudimentary medical education had been available in England and Wales since 1123 but many early medics obtained their skills through apprenticeships or by on the job observation with more experienced doctors and practitioners.

In the sixteenth and seventeenth centuries, medical education and training was patchy; some was formal such as when a bespoke facility for medical training was established but prior to that, medical teaching and training was erratic to say the least.

Details on when and where early medical training began can be found in appendix 1.

The Medical Act 1858 was fundamental to professional training in medical practice and it was through the General Medical Council that the publication of the medical register was established. In the late eighteenth century more than half of all those practising had served an apprenticeship to learn their trade. Apothecaries began to train as surgeons; surgeons began to take university degrees to qualify as physicians and many apothecaries were also members of the Royal College of Surgeons. Only a small number of teaching hospitals existed during the early Victorian era but these gradually increased in later years with the result that the number of doctors being trained at universities also significantly increased.

Some biographical details of doctors who went to either Oxford or Cambridge universities can be found in the respective alumni volumes for each university. The records of the individual colleges within these universities may also contain information and could include details about those who did not graduate. Other university alumni contain similar information for graduating students.

Anatomy and body-snatching

From the early nineteenth century there were significant advances in science and medicine at a time when scientific and religious ideas often clashed over what was morally correct. The study of anatomy had always had a fractious history because religion traditionally dictated that dissection of human bodies was an offence in canon law and could easily lead to misunderstandings of the human anatomy based only on limited evidence.

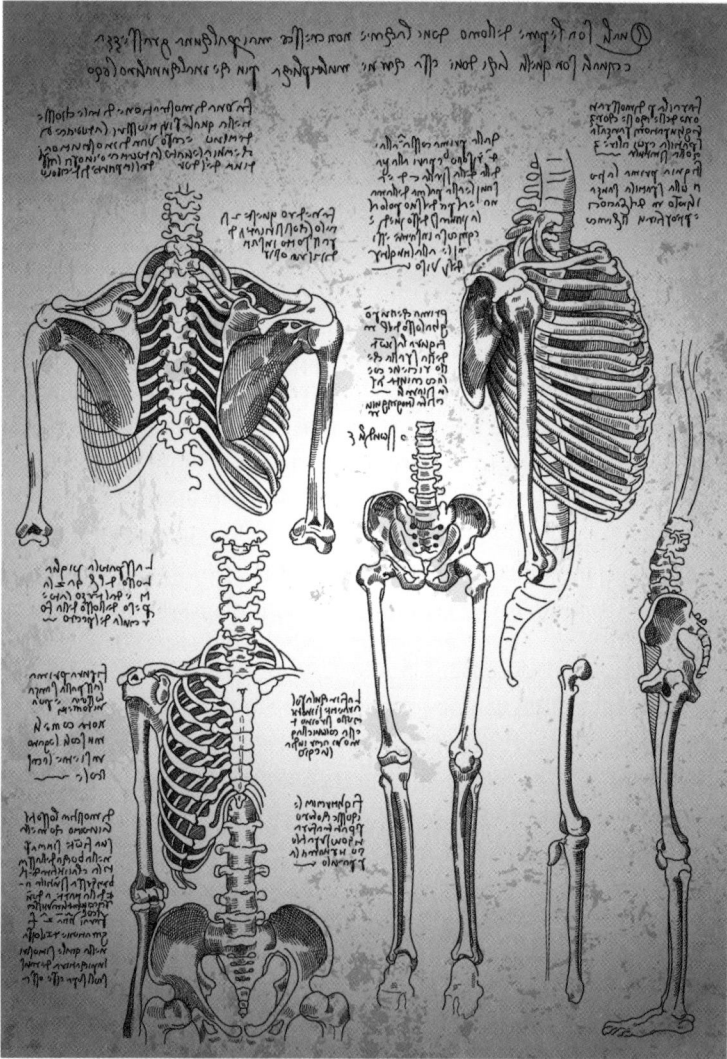

Diagram of human anatomy at the time of Leonardo da Vinci

In 1565 Elizabeth I signed the charter for anatomies. This gave the College of Physicians the exclusive right to obtain four bodies of hanged criminals annually from Tyburn to be used for anatomy lessons. The government passed the Murder Act 1751 which prohibited the burial of the bodies of executed murderers, so their bodies were passed on to the teaching hospitals for the advancement of medical science. As a result medical students had a supply of corpses which meant that the study of anatomy through dissection played a major role in the training of both doctors and surgeons.

The opening of new medical schools meant that even with bodies of executed murderers being available, demand still outstripped supply. Buried bodies were often exhumed and sold without restriction though the practice was despised by the public. Cemetery owners and family mourners began to take measures to prevent exhumations by installing railings, gates, cages and mausoleums to protect dead bodies. However, the increasing demand for bodies created a profitable black market and body-snatching became routine.

Body-snatching was defined as the act of secretly removing corpses from burial grounds. A common purpose of body-snatching was to sell corpses for dissection or anatomy lectures in the medical schools. A related act was that of grave-robbing, the uncovering of a tomb or crypt to steal artefacts or personal effects that had been buried with the deceased. Grave-robbing differs from body-snatching in that the crime of grave-robbing did not involve stealing the corpse itself.

A nightwatchman disturbs a body-snatcher who has dropped the stolen corpse he had been carrying in a hamper, while the anatomist runs away.

Body-snatchers usually dug around the head end of a grave at night with a wooden spade – they made less noise than a metal one. When the coffin was located, they broke the head end open, put a rope round the corpse and dragged the body out. In many cases this was unencumbered as most graves were shallow, particularly in the multi-occupied graves in over-crowded churchyards.

An article in the *Lancet* described another method of body-snatching which was less apparent and slightly more sophisticated. Turf was removed around fifteen feet away from the head of the grave and a tunnel dug up to the coffin. The head end of the coffin would be broken open and the corpse pulled through the tunnel. The turf was then replaced and any relatives watching the graves would not notice the remote disturbance. The number of empty coffins subsequently discovered in cemeteries and churchyards showed beyond any doubt that this type of body-snatching was frequently undertaken and remained undetected.

High walls with watchtowers around cemeteries became common features, supposedly built to deter body-snatchers. Many watchtowers existed from the early 1820s. Some unscrupulous watchmen were associates of the

Cemetery watchtower and surrounding wall

body-snatchers as they were paid to turn a blind eye during the illegal exhumations; some gravediggers, sextons and even some undertakers were also among those helping the body-snatchers. Some cemetery authorities implemented tighter controls where watchmen were required to have two or three dogs roaming the cemeteries at night as a deterrent.

Body-snatchers in the eighteenth and nineteenth centuries had an unpopular reputation and they were rejected by virtually every level of society. In some areas even the teachers or surgeons associated with dissection were thought of in the same way. The general public remained very much against dissection for both moral and religious reasons. To try and prevent the theft of bodies, heavy iron mort safes were laid over the grave or bars of iron were fixed across the coffin and bedded in the earth before the graves were filled in. Poorer families who could not afford these measures placed items on their loved one's grave so they could establish if a grave had been disturbed. But despite great lengths taken to secure graves, there was no successful method to stop the body-snatchers.

The most well-known body snatchers or *resurrectionists* as they were known were Burke and Hare from Edinburgh but the case of the Bethnal Green Gang from London in the early 1830s led to the passing of the Anatomy Act of 1832 giving legal recognition of the rights of a corpse. This Act allowed unclaimed bodies and those donated by relatives to be used for the study of anatomy. Licences granted by the Home Secretary were required before anyone could teach anatomy. Only one or two teachers at each institution received licences. Four government inspectors of anatomy regulated the licensed teachers, who each reported the details of each body being dissected in the area that they were responsible for to the Home Secretary. After 1832 body-snatching was significantly reduced but not totally eliminated.

Records of the Anatomy Inspectorate relating to the lawful acquisition of bodies and the granting of licences to practise anatomy are in MH 74 at The National Archives covering the period 1832 to 1971 and include registers and correspondence files. The register details all bodies available to anatomy schools and is known as the Anatomy Register which more importantly lists all those whose bodies were actually dissected in schools of anatomy. If you have difficulty locating a burial or grave for your ancestor, it could be worth checking the anatomy register.

If a body-snatcher exists within your ancestry, you will not be able to identify them by occupation as many of them had respectable day jobs, so lateral thinking and some detective work is needed to identify anyone who was a body-snatcher.

Contemporary newspapers are a good place to start research because they will provide gruesome details of any trials or prosecutions. They will also contain information about rewards offered for the apprehension of body-snatchers. Local record offices may be able to help with records such as Quarter Sessions where cases of body-snatching mainly exist.

If your ancestor died as a pauper in a workhouse, a house of correction or a gaol, or was a criminal sentenced to death by hanging and dissection, then a search could be simpler. Under the 1832 Anatomy Act bodies could be purchased from the poor law authorities. There will not be burials recorded in the parish registers or workhouse burial grounds but the records of the board of guardians may suggest a body was sold to a hospital or teaching school. Such transactions were common. Fees paid to workhouses will be shown in any surviving workhouse accounts or in the union *dead book*.

Records of medical professionals

If you have a medical professional within your ancestry, finding information about them will depend on where he or she lived or worked and what discipline of medicine they practised. There are more sources available from the early nineteenth century than in earlier periods. The efforts of the various professions in organisation helped to enhance their status, so even if you cannot find any information about your ancestor, you should be able to get a clear picture of the type of work they did from the records of their professional bodies, hospitals or even medical museums including:

- Anaesthesia Heritage Centre
- Army Medical Services Museum
- British Dental Association Museum

- British Optical Association Museum
- Red Cross Museum
- Florence Nightingale Museum
- Royal London Hospital Museum.

Physicians

The Royal College of Physicians of London was founded in 1518 by a Royal Charter granted by Henry VIII and is the oldest medical college in England; its aim was to establish an academy for physicians rather than continue as a trade guild. Physicians needed to become the best educated within the medical world so a university degree became the minimum required to gain a licence. All candidates were required to take an oral examination to demonstrate that they had been classically educated. Fellowship of the college made them full voting members and this status required a degree from either Oxford or Cambridge universities. During the first four hundred years of its existence, women were excluded from being licensed or becoming members.

The term 'physician' originally meant a medical practitioner who diagnosed internal disorders, as opposed to carrying out surgery or dispensing medicine. Not all physicians belonged to the Royal College. The college created the first standard list of medicines which regulated the formulation of all medicines from 1618 until 1864.

Until 1617 drugs and medicines in common use were sold by apothecaries and grocers. The preparation of prescriptions was the sole responsibility of apothecaries and they were required to dispense them with accuracy. The wardens of the Worshipful Society of Apothecaries and the censors of the College of Physicians examining the shops of apothecaries went a long way to standardise drug production. Initially this happened within a seven-mile radius of the City of London but later the coverage expanded. During an inspection they had the power to destroy all drugs which were not properly prepared.

Although revised editions of the *Pharmacopoeia* were issued in 1621, 1632, 1639, and 1677, it was not until the 1721 edition that significant revisions were made. In the 1721 edition many of the remedies previously included and in regular use were omitted, including some no longer in vogue in London but still in use in other areas of the country. A further edition published in 1746, simplified older formulae by eliminating the use of superfluous ingredients. Later editions tended to simplify formulae even further.

Royal College of Physicians – Munk's Roll

The Royal College of Physicians maintained biographies of members between 1518 and 1825 but after 1825 only the biographies of the fellows exist. William Munk researched and compiled entries for all fellow and licentiate voting and non-voting members. This information is in the Munk's roll. The roll is still updated and maintained to this day and currently known as *Inspiring Physicians*. In 1855, Munk presented a leather-bound volume to the college. It was a thoroughly researched collection of biographies covering the period 1518 to 1600. Later that year he gave the college a second volume, covering 1601 to 1700 and in 1856, a third volume was presented covering the period up to 1825. Editions after 1825 were limited to fellows and were entitled *Lives of the Fellows of the Royal College of Physicians of London.*

Munk never intended the roll to be published but in 1860 he agreed to the publication and a year later the first edition became available. It was agreed that the college roll would be printed under the direction of Dr Munk at the expense of the college. Munk's Roll is an invaluable resource for family historians and can be searched online. See website details in the appendices.

An example of the information is shown in the entry for Thomas West:

Thomas West, M.D., was born in Northamptonshire, and was originally of Exeter college, Oxford, as a member of which he took the degree of Bachelor of Arts 17th October 1687; but then removing to Merton college, proceeded A.M. 13th November 1691; M.B. 29th April 1693; M.D. 25th June 1696. He was admitted a Candidate of the College of Physicians 23rd December 1717; and a Fellow 22nd December 1718. He was Treasurer in 1721 and 1722; Censor, 1725, 1729; and dying suddenly at his house in Red Lion-square, 17th August 1738, was buried in the chapel of Merton college, Oxford, where he is thus commemorated:

Here, near the remains of his first wife,

Catherine, daughter of Dr. Lydall,

who died Decr ye 16, a.d. 1705,

lieth

the body of Thomas West, M.D.

Fellow of the College of Physicians, and formerly Fellow of this College,

who departed this life the seventeenth day of August, in the year of our Lord

1738, aged 70 years.

Ecclesiastical licences

Physicians practising in the London area between 1529 and the late 1760s can be traced in ecclesiastical licensing records held mainly in local or diocesan record offices. *Raach's Directory of English County Physicians 1603–1643* was compiled from surviving ecclesiastical records. The licences were normally granted through the consistory courts in each diocese.

The Wellcome Institute for the History of Medicine holds published transcript records for known bishops' licences issued to episcopal medical licentiates up to 1700.

The licences for some dioceses have also been printed:

- Canterbury licences (general) 1568–1646
- medical practitioners in the diocese of London 1529–1725 (1935)
- lists of schoolmasters and surgeons licensed by the Bishop of Hereford 1683–1835

There may well be other printed volumes available.

The College of Physicians' archive

The College of Physicians' archive contains diaries, letters, and casebooks of medical practitioners and students including papers of influential doctors such as Elizabeth Garrett Anderson, along with records of places physicians have worked, including hospitals, dispensaries and workhouses.

The archives are located at 11 St Andrews Place, London NW1 4LE. If you need to access rare book and archive collections, you will need to register as a researcher. There is a series of research guides of interest to family historians. Detailed links can be found in the website listing appendix.

To use the archives to the best advantage, you will need to have basic information about your physician ancestor including:

- full name
- where they lived
- any hospitals they worked in
- their dates of birth/death
- possible dates of employment.

The archive also comprises collections of various individuals and institutions, dating from the fourteenth century to the present day which were acquired by the Royal College of Physicians of Edinburgh and are listed alphabetically. Much of the Edinburgh archive is available to view online – see link in website listing appendix.

Apothecaries

The Apothecaries Act of 1815 introduced a compulsory apprenticeship term and formal qualifications for apothecaries from the Society of Apothecaries. It also gave the society the power to licence and regulate medical practitioners throughout England and Wales. The society retained this role until the late twentieth century.

The Worshipful Society of Apothecaries, a City of London livery company, ranks fifty-eighth in order of precedence. They were granted a Royal Charter by James I. Prior to this, the London apothecaries were members of the Grocers' Company established in 1345 and described as the *Mistery of Grossers, Pepperers and Apothecaries.* After their independence the apothecaries contested the monopoly held by the College of Physicians. In 1704 after a legal battle overturning earlier precedence, the House of Lords granted apothecaries the right to practise medicine so apothecaries became the forerunners of the present-day general practitioner and family doctor.

Typical interior of an apothecary's shop.

Throughout history the Society of Apothecaries has pioneered specialist medical knowledge, general practice and specialisation in obstetrics, occupational medicine, and legal and forensic medicine. The original licences issued to members meant holders were Licentiates of the Society.

When the General Medical Council was established, the Society of Apothecaries' licentiateship was accepted as a qualification. After 1885 their examinations included surgery and gynaecology which were two required skills determined by the Medical Act of 1886. But the society was not recognised as a provider of primary medical qualifications by the General Medical Council.

After the Apothecaries' Act 1815 the society also set the qualifying examination for pharmacy dispensers. In 1928 the society instituted a postgraduate qualification in midwifery and instigated diplomas in other specialist subjects not offered by the universities or other medical bodies. The records of the Society of Apothecaries are held by the society at their hall but the archive is run by volunteers so visits are by appointment only.

The collection includes:

- the apprentice-bindings 1617–1836 which show dates of birth
- freedom admission registers 1617–1890
- candidates' qualification books 1815–1939
- alphabetical list of the licentiates, 1815–1840.

The last item shows their addresses and the dates they qualified; a copy is also available at the Society of Genealogists' library.

The professional career paths of qualified medical practitioners may be traced using either the medical directory or medical register, which have been published annually.

Surgeons

The definition of a surgeon is *a person who performs operations with the use of surgical instruments*. The Company of Surgeons was established in 1745 and records and archives exist from then up to the present day.

The Barbers' Company was originally established in 1308 and included surgeons from about 1312. Barbers and surgeons had co-existed for some time – the common element being working with sharp implements. Barbers attached to monasteries began to undertake minor surgery and the skills they learned were passed to the outside barbers.

The Fellowship of Surgeons was a London trade guild which developed alongside the Barbers' Company from around 1435 and claimed the right to practise surgery; this led to ongoing disputes with the barbers. The situation was temporarily resolved in 1462 when the Barbers' Company was granted a royal charter which gave it the power to regulate the practice of surgery within the City of London and more importantly to enforce professional standards.

The roles of both barbers and surgeons in London were combined after an Act of Parliament in 1540 which established the Company of Barbers and Surgeons of London. This Act stated that no surgeon was to undertake the work of a barber and vice versa – although both were allowed to extract teeth. The 1540 Act also granted surgeons four executed bodies annually for the purpose of anatomical training as was the case with the physicians. The barber's pole with its red-and-white spiralling stripes denotes surgeons (red) and barbers (white).

In urban barber-surgeons' shops it was common to see patients undergoing surgical procedures next to customers having a haircut or shave; however, in villages and poorer establishments in towns, patients underwent surgical procedures in a dedicated room in the surgeon's own house. This made sense because not only were surgeons aware of the pain they could cause, they had limited knowledge about the effects an operation would have on their patient, so using a dedicated room was the best for all. Surgeons only tackled amputations and other major operations when there was no other option.

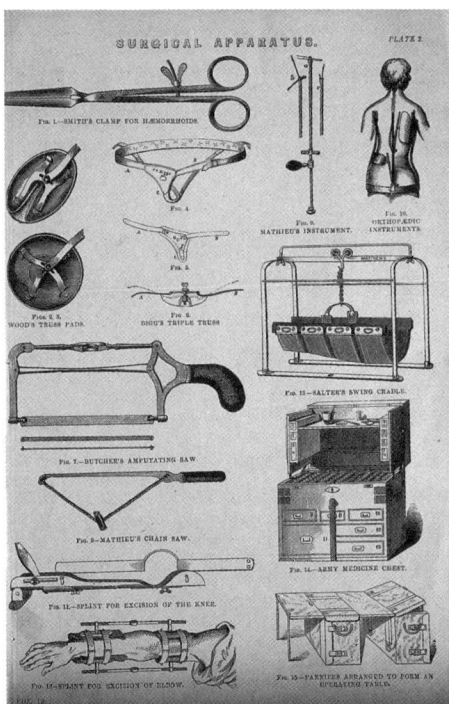

A range of surgical instruments many of which are still used today in modern form.

To become a member of the company, candidates served a seven-year apprenticeship with an experienced barber-surgeon. They would assist with surgical care and gain practical experience in setting bones and stitching wounds. Once the apprenticeship was completed they were examined to demonstrate their skills and abilities and if they passed the examination, they paid a membership fee and joined the company. In 1745 the surgeons left the company and in 1800 the Royal College of Surgeons was established. Members and fellows of the Royal College of Surgeons use the designation of Mr, Miss or Mrs, a custom dating back to the sixteenth century but now with greater kudos.

In 1796, the surgeons acquired property in Lincoln's Inn Fields where their business was carried out. That same year, the government moved the museum of surgeon John Hunter to the premises. John Hunter (1728–1793) was a remarkable Scottish surgeon and during his lifetime, he acquired a superb collection of anatomical and medical specimens. After his death in 1793, the Company of Surgeons amalgamated this into their holdings having agreed to make the museum available to medical professionals and students. This establishment became known as the Hunterian Museum and still exists today.

Their charter of 1843 enabled the society to create higher levels of qualifi-cations and the fellowship of the college. As new developments expanded surgical possibilities, the college examinations became more thorough with the introduction of specialist subjects and from the 1880s their exams were held jointly with the Royal College of Physicians.

The records of the Barber-Surgeons' Company of London remain with the Barbers' Company but the registers of apprentices 1657–1786 and of admissions to freedom 1522–1801 are available through the City of London Joint Archive Service. The admission registers of the former Company of Surgeons 1745–1796 remain with the Royal College of Surgeons.

Examination records for surgeons originated with the establishment of the Company of Surgeons after it separated from the Company of Barbers. The records give an insight into changes and advancement of knowledge and attitudes within the profession, as well as giving the examination results.

The college's own archives and manuscripts cover material relating to medicine and surgery from the sixteenth to twentieth century and include:

- hospital records
- lecture notes
- minute books
- records of various medical clubs and societies
- personal papers and case notes which include diaries, drawings and photographs
- records of admissions to the Company of Surgeons, 1745–1800
- general examination records from 1800 onwards not including specialty exams
- college membership and fellowship records from c1870.

Royal College of Surgeons – Plarr's Lives

Plarr's *Lives of the Fellows of the Royal College of Surgeons of England* is a collection of biographies of deceased fellows of the college. Similar in purpose to the physicians' Munk's Roll, it is a unique record of surgeons covering the period from the establishment of fellowships in 1843 onwards – but also covers lives of some of the prominent earlier surgeons. Victor Plarr (1863–1929) was a poet and writer. Having graduated from Oxford University he worked as a librarian at the Royal College of Surgeons. *Plarr's Lives* was originally a series of printed books – the first two were published in 1930 with seven further volumes produced later; the last printed edition was published in 2005. These can now be searched online (see link in website listings) which means you can now search the biographies of nearly 10,000 surgeons and then find out what books, papers, artefacts or other materials the college holds that relate to that surgeon.

Pharmacists

As London grew and expanded, there was an increase in the manufacture and dispensing of medicines. Chemists and druggists appeared in many urban areas outside London from as early as the end of the medieval period. During and after the Industrial Revolution they would typically occupy main street positions; as well as mixing and dispensing medicines they sold cosmetics and other such items. These chemists and druggists were not regulated and without a national organisation there was no awareness of pharmacy as a profession, notwithstanding the established apothecaries. Most of the chemists and druggists focused on the demands of their customers often specialising in different products including chemicals for the developing of photographs to making matches.

The various established professional bodies supporting the medical world were aware that the chemists and druggists were untrained and unregulated and there was a great desire amongst the medical profession to regulate their status. In 1841 a Medical Reform bill was proposed which set out to prevent chemists and druggists from dispensing medicines unless medically qualified.

Pharmacy dates to the first half of the nineteenth century as a profession. In Britain pharmacy really began with the establishment of the Pharmaceutical Society of Great Britain in 1841 and membership in 1842 was nearly 2,000. Their Royal Charter granted in 1843 helped with the transition from a trade to a profession. The Royal Society focused on education by advancing pharmacy and giving protection to those in business as chemists and druggists.

Once established, the Royal Pharmaceutical Society had a clear mandate to encourage reform with the aid of legislation, so the 1852 Pharmacy Act established a register of pharmaceutical chemists, but it had its shortcomings because registration was voluntary and not linked to a compulsory education programme or examination. The 1868 Pharmacy and Poisons Act regulated pharmacy education; pharmacists who wanted to dispense medicines had to be on the society's register which meant they had to pass the society's examinations. Included within the same Act was the regulation which made it unlawful for any person to sell or keep a shop for retailing, dispensing or compounding medicines, or to assume the title chemist, druggist, pharmacist or dispensing chemist unless they were registered under the terms of the Act.

Following a legal case in 1880, companies as well as individuals could operate pharmacy businesses. Pharmacy companies began to appear; by the turn of the twentieth century *Boots the Chemist* had around 250 branches throughout the country. Chain pharmacies could not be run by unqualified businessmen and legislation in 1908 ensured that a qualified pharmacist was on the board of directors of companies and acted as the superintendent pharmacist with each branch being directed by a qualified pharmacist.

Victorian pharmacies

Victorian pharmacies did far more than dispense prescribed medicines. Their main source of income was from the sale of patent medicines, veterinary products and household items including ink, cosmetics and hair products. The ingredients of the medicines were mainly plants and minerals; this centuries-old tradition continued well into the twentieth century. Both prescribed and patent medicines were made up in the dispensary by the chemist. Chemists' shops were always recognizable by large glass vessels filled with coloured liquid which were prominently displayed.

You may find prescription books and recipe books from Victorian pharmacies deposited in record offices or living museum research archives. From these you can build up a picture of the medicines supplied and their costs together with the names of those for whom the medicines were prescribed. However, the majority of the population still had to rely on patent medicines enticed by extensive, eye-catching advertising.

Until the late 1800s most available drugs were based on herbs or the extraction of ingredients from arboreal and botanical sources. Notwithstanding all the advances made in the Victorian era, there remained only a few drugs available for treating diseases by the start of the twentieth century including:

- digitalis extracted from foxgloves; stimulated the cardiac muscles and used to treat general heart conditions
- quinine taken from the bark of the cinchona tree; used in the treatment of malaria

- ipecacuanha used to treat dysentery
- aspirin extracted from willow bark; and used in the general treatment of fever.

Significant advances in research were being undertaken to discover new drugs from the early 1900s using chemical methods; this heralded the start of the pharmaceutical industry. Most of the drugs manufactured this way were only used for therapeutic purposes rather than being a cure for disease. A list of some of the drugs which had been discovered and were available from the pharmacists can be seen at appendix 2.

Pharmaceutical Society register

Since its establishment in 1841, the Royal Pharmaceutical Society has maintained a register of its members but because registration was not compulsory until 1868, the initial registers are incomplete. The registers only include basic information including full name, date of registration, type of examination and sometimes a death date. In the early days only those pharmacists who ran chemists' shops could be full members of the society; others were known as associates. This categorisation changed after 1872. In some instances widows had taken over the running of a chemist's shop after the death of their husbands and in 1868 there were over two hundred women in the register; it was not until 1869 that women were allowed to take the examinations. Even then some were refused membership until 1879 when petitions were made and the society relented.

There are two journals which might be of interest to researchers in this field. The *Pharmaceutical Journal* began in 1841 and is the official publication of the society; it includes examination pass lists and obituaries as well as anyone struck off the register. The *Chemist and Druggist* which came later in 1858 includes trade advertisements and information on sales of businesses and bankruptcies. The Royal Pharmaceutical Society library has good runs of both of these journals as well as other information which will enable a researcher to find more information about the lives of its members.

People sometimes get confused about the different occupational names of those involved in this trade so a little clarification follows.

- in earlier times, pharmacists adopted the word chemist and druggist
- today chemists and druggists are referred to as pharmacists
- chemists are not always involved in the same disciplines
- dispensers are not pharmacists
- dispensers prepare and issue medicines under a pharmacist's supervision
- druggists are involved in the manufacture of drugs, not dispensing prescriptions.

The registers of the Pharmaceutical Society were published annually from 1869 up to 2010. The society also published lists of members, associates and apprentices from 1841 to 1868 and the register of approved premises annually from 1936 to 2010.

The Royal Pharmaceutical Society museum and library have a complete set of the registers, as well as various other resources to help with your research. The library will provide a free copy of their information sheet *Tracing people and premises in pharmacy*, which explains the sources available and lists other possible research centres. They also operate a paid research enquiry service which is often busy so you may not receive an immediate reply. You can also personally visit the library and undertake your own research but you need to book in advance.

The Pharmaceutical Historian has been published by the British Society for the History of Pharmacy since 1967 – and since 1972 on a quarterly basis. The society originated from a committee of the Royal Pharmaceutical Society and *aims to include the promotion of historical studies related to pharmacy, the advancement of knowledge and propagation of understanding of the history of pharmacy and publication of the research work of pharmaceutical historians.*

General practitioners

The Royal College of General Practitioners was established in 1952 and therefore only holds a limited amount of information about GPs after that date. Records of GPs prior to 1952 are held by the other appropriate professional bodies.

Medical directories

The annual publication of the Medical Directory, beginning in 1845, and the Medical Register which began in 1859 are the starting points for research. They contain lots of information such as…

- names
- addresses
- qualifications
- medical school
- any publications by a doctor.

The medical register was a complete list of practitioners, but the medical directory was a commercial directory for which an entry was not compulsory; information can be found in one but not the other, so searching both is essential. There is an obituary section but sometimes notice of doctors' deaths is not published until a year or two after the actual death.

Medical school records

The medical directory contains a full list and recognised abbreviations of the various medical qualifications. Both the register and directory will indicate the medical school your ancestor attended. The easiest way to find more information is to contact the school or the university archive directly. The alumni of the medical schools or universities should include information about the career of an individual. Some schools also publish obituaries or news in their regular bulletins or journals.

The term general practitioner (GP) was not used until the 1820s and then only by apothecaries. Doctors would have belonged to the colleges of physicians or surgeons or would have most probably obtained licentiateship of the Society of Apothecaries. The medical registers or directory should contain information about them.

Dentists

The science of dentistry developed between 1650 and 1800 and that was when dentistry evolved from a trade to a profession. In the mid-nineteenth century there was no organisation or code of practice for the dental profession. The number of dentists had increased but without controls, there was no way to prevent malpractice and incompetence.

By the 1870s leading dentists had established the Dental Reform Committee which campaigned for legislation to regulate dentistry establishing the British Dental Association in 1880. Most of their early work involved prosecuting dentists who were in breach of the 1878 Dentists' Act. The Dentists' Act of 1921 created the Dental Board of the United Kingdom to administer the dentists' register when the BDA became the leading consultative body.

Dentistry continued to evolve from the late eighteenth century and throughout the nineteenth century. Until the late nineteenth century, dentists usually learned their trade through apprenticeship. The Royal College of Surgeons actually introduced the Licence in Dental Surgery in 1860.

A dentistry timeline can be found in appendix 3.

The dentists' register

From 1879 the register of dentists includes:

- full name
- address
- date of registration
- name of the qualification
- where the qualification was obtained.

Those included in the register had to be qualified or show they had practised dentistry before 1879, either as specialists or in conjunction with surgery, pharmacy or another medical discipline. Only those on the register could call themselves *dentist* or *dental surgeon*. However, many highly skilled practitioners continued to practise without registration, so from 1921 the law changed allowing only registered dentists to practise.

A complete run of the register is held by the British Dental Association museum and archives. The *British Journal of Dental Science* may include obituaries for an ancestor and can also be found at the museum. There are some interesting articles and listings for those who were members of the Royal Army Dental Corps dating from around 1856. The Museum of Military Medicine at Aldershot holds editions from 1856–1909. For those with ancestors who qualified between 1911 and 1937, the Medical and Dental Students' Register includes lists of all those registered between the two dates. This is held at the Wellcome Library.

The *British Dental Journal* is highly regarded throughout the dentistry profession. Editions from 1950 onwards are available online. It was originally established in 1872 as the *Monthly Review of Dental Surgery* and renamed *Journal of the British Dental Association* in 1881, before obtaining its current title in 1904.

Nurses and midwives

Prior to the Reformation nursing was generally administered by religious bodies with both male and female nurses. After the dissolution of the monasteries, some secular hospitals were reinstated although most nursing care was then carried out by untrained women. Doctors' assistants undertook duties that are the nurses' responsibilities in today's hospitals. The situation changed little until the 1850s when several Anglican nursing sisterhoods began to improve the standard of nursing care.

In workhouse infirmaries the nursing staff were often untrained female inmates; in the larger town and city workhouses, some experienced nurses were members of staff and some employed Nightingale nurses.

General nursing before the Victorian era was not a particularly well-respected profession and standards were often low. Elizabeth Fry set up the Institute of Nursing Sisters in the 1840s to try to improve standards, but it was really Florence Nightingale in the aftermath of the Crimean War who set the gold standard. Before 1860, the role of a nurse was similar to that of a domestic housemaid because nurses had little medical education beyond knowing how to make poultices, keep the wards clean and attend to patients' care needs.

Nightingale nurses

Significant changes in general nursing care occurred after the Crimean War inspired by the work of Florence Nightingale. The Nightingale Training

School for Nurses was established at St Thomas' Hospital London in 1860 as part of her campaign to improve nursing and health care. The school was the first open institution to provide professional nursing and midwifery training.

Nightingale nurse's badge

Florence Nightingale was considered a national hero because of her work during the Crimean War; she became aware that many of soldiers she was caring for were dying from infectious diseases rather than from the effects of their battle wounds. She deduced that the main reasons for this were overcrowding and malnutrition so her solutions proposed better ventilation and sanitation; these two basic functions became the focus of her reports about the conditions at the military hospitals.

All this came about because she and thirty-eight volunteer women nurses were sent to the battlefields of the Crimea. When Florence arrived at Scutari, she discovered that poor care of wounded soldiers was being delivered by an overworked and inadequate medical staff. Medicines were in short supply, hygiene was neglected and fatal infections were common. During the winter of 1854 over 4000 soldiers died, not from their injuries but mostly from infections including typhus, typhoid, cholera, and dysentery. She also became acutely aware of official apathy to the situation. After her new basic improvements were instigated, death rates of patients were significantly reduced. When she returned to Britain, she gave evidence to the Royal Commission on the health of the army.

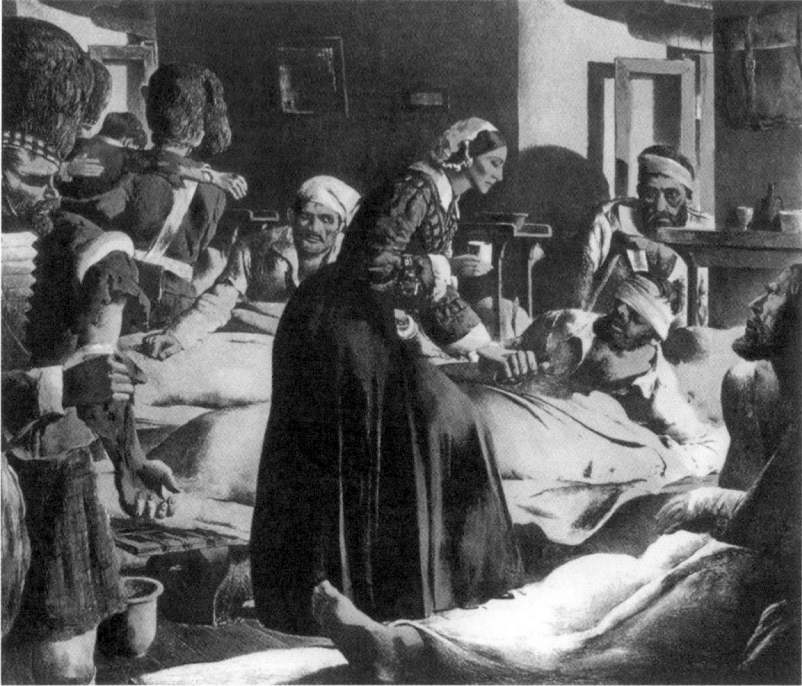

Florence Nightingale administering to soldiers during the Crimean War

Her experiences in Crimea influenced her later career and consequently she turned her attention to the better design and layout of hospitals. However, Florence Nightingale's enduring contribution was her role in establishing the modern nursing profession. Inspired by her work in Crimea, a public fund was established in 1855 to raise money so she could continue her groundbreaking work.

Florence initially received £45,000 (equivalent to about £2.5 million today) for the establishment of the Nightingale Training School at St Thomas' Hospital. The first fully-trained Nightingale nurses began work in May 1865 at the Liverpool workhouse infirmary. Prior to then, no provincial workhouses had ever employed trained nurses. Twelve qualified nurses and eighteen probationers from the school were sent to the infirmaries. Every nurse who graduated from the training school made the *Nightingale*

Pledge which was a statement of the ethics and principles of the nursing profession.

As part of her legacy, the Red Cross instituted the Florence Nightingale Medal in 1912, which is awarded every two years to nurses or nursing aides for *exceptional courage and devotion to the wounded, sick or disabled or to civilian victims of a conflict or disaster* or *exemplary services or a creative and pioneering spirit in the areas of public health or nursing education*. An alphabetical list of recipients of the medal can be searched on Wikipedia (see link in website listings).

When Florence's school was established the typical training was for one year. Students attended classes and actually cared for patients at St. Thomas' Hospital under supervision. Up to thirty students were accepted each year based upon their social class. Common class students received a small amount of money plus a placement in a home or institution upon completion of their course, whereas upper-class students would be given the opportunity to assist at the school itself. Uniforms were provided and upon graduation the nurses would meet Florence Nightingale in person. Florence kept meticulous notes about her students and placed particular importance upon character because if this was questionable then the final certification of a nurse would be opposed. Many Nightingale nurses ultimately held senior positions as matrons or nursing superintendents in major hospitals.

The Nightingale nurses not only served at St. Thomas' Hospital, but they were also sent to other institutions in groups to carry out nursing reforms. Some groups went to Canada and Australia as well as to hospitals in England.

Probationers were provided with living accommodation. When the new St Thomas' Hospital opened in 1871, the Nightingale Nurses' Home was also provided. The Nightingale Fellowship was founded in 1928 and the distinctive Nightingale badge was first presented in 1925. The Nightingale Fellowship was established to embrace all qualified Nightingale nurses and published its first journal in 1928. It also held gatherings twice a year. A benevolent fund was also established due largely to the generosity of a former Nightingale nurses.

As advances were made in medical techniques so nurses' training also developed; the training period was increased in order to achieve higher levels of expertise. Until the early twentieth century, a hospital was frequently considered the last resort for the patient; the nature of infectious diseases and their control with antiseptics, although understood, still meant that the risk of acquiring infection in hospital was high.

The Nightingale School of Nursing amalgamated with the Thomas Guy and Lewisham School of Nursing in 1991 to form Nightingale and Guy's College of Nursing and Midwifery. In 1992 it was renamed the Nightingale and Guy's College of Health.

The records of the Nightingale Training School are deposited with the London Metropolitan Archives.

The Nightingale Training School admissions registers cover the period 1860–1920.

Full details of both these records can be found at appendix 4.

Other significant school of nursing records are held by King's College London Archives:

- King's College Hospital School of Nursing, 1885–1998
- Dulwich Hospital, 1917–1967
- St Saviour's Infirmary, [1890]-1931
- Lewisham School of Nursing, 1897–1981
- other nursing records from hospitals into the mid-twentieth century.

St John's House Anglican Nursing Sisterhood
This was an Anglican nursing sisterhood established in 1848 to provided nurses to care for the sick in their own homes. The sisterhood became responsible for nursing at both King's College Hospital in 1856 and Charing Cross Hospital ten years later. The St John's House Maternity Home was opened in 1877, originally in Chelsea but relocated to Battersea in 1883.

In 1883 a dispute over nursing administration at King's College Hospital resulted in the mass resignation of the sisters and most of them then established the Community of the Nursing Sisters of St John the Divine, but St John's House continued to suffer because of lack of recruitment. In 1920 it was attached to St Thomas' Hospital which became the centre for their nurses who wanted to become private nurses.

Their records are held at the London Metropolitan Archives and details can be seen in appendix 5.

Many training hospitals also hold records of the nurses they trained and employed although it may not be as easy to find information on the employed nurses. Voluntary hospitals and workhouse infirmaries in some areas established training schools whose superintendents were usually trained by the Nightingale School. Training was also undertaken to provide district nurses to care for the sick poor in the community through the Queen's Institute of District Nursing.

Civilian nurses

Before 1921 when nursing registration commenced, the only records are likely to be in the hospital archives of where the nurses were employed. Staff registers broadly include the same information irrespective of where your ancestor was employed. Hospital records can include:

- full name
- age
- sponsor or person recommending them
- previous posting
- where they went after leaving
- character and ability.

After 1890 you may find more information about nurses as probationers or students and details of their training. Initially they may also appear in hospital minute books, more so if the nurse applied for a senior appointment. In many hospitals nursing committees existed which dealt with all aspects of a nurse's career including appointments, resignations, dismissals, pensions and other matters.

If your ancestor was a Nightingale nurse the records include a registration number, their marital status as well as their training report and the appointments held during the first three years after training. You may also be able to locate details of later employment.

If nurses were appointed to poor law infirmaries, then there should be information about her in the minutes of the board of guardians for the union in which they worked. There should also be a record within the poor law commission records held at The National Archives in series MH12 which includes letters and other correspondence between the commission and the union boards and may include an application form. Individual union staff listings are also given in series MH9 where it is possible to find the name of the nurse, when appointed/left/dismissed and their wages. The guardian minute books should also record resignations and may well contain other information about staff during their daily work, including any complaints and reprimands made during service.

After about 1870 and up to the demise of the particular workhouse, staff registers may also exist and these will include details of the infirmary nurses. The information about all nurses who were trained after 1897 is likely to mirror that of hospital nurses. This assumes, of course, that records of the particular union still exist.

State registration of nurses

The General Nursing Council was set up in 1921 and maintained a register of nurses effectively establishing State Registration (SRN) which followed the Nurses' Registration Act of 1919. A general register with separate sections for male nurses, fever nurses, mental nurses and paediatric nurses was introduced. Competent, experienced but untrained nurses were allowed to register in 1921, but thereafter, all nurses were required to complete an approved three-year training programme culminating in State Registration. In 1943 a roll of assistant nurses was also established and these two rolls up to 1968 are available to view online on Ancestry.co.uk.

The Register of Nurses was produced annually until 1940 and lists all nurses alphabetically:

- surname and forenames
- date of registration
- number
- residential address
- where and when qualified.

State enrolled nurses

The Nurses' Act 1943 established a new nursing category – State Enrolled Nurse (SEN). You can find records for SENs in the roll of nurses. The General Nursing Council kept the roll and set the syllabus for the two-year course. The registers can be accessed at the Wellcome Library and Royal College of Nurses Archives. The National Archives also holds the records of the General Nursing Council for England and Wales which includes:

- the Register of Nurses 1921–1973
- the Roll of Nurses 1944–1973
- digitised register for the ten years 1973–1983.

It is still possible to locate information about trained nurses prior to compulsory registration. The Register of Trained Nurses exists for 1891, 1892 and 1896 and was published by the Royal British Nurses Association, established in 1887. The registers are available at the Wellcome Library.

In 1916 the Royal College of Nursing became the recognised professional association for nurses, later becoming their trade union. You may be able to locate information about a nurse between 1916 and 1923 including:

- name
- year of joining
- where trained.

General Nursing Council

The General Nursing Council was established for England and Wales with separate councils for Scotland and Ireland. Each was responsible for keeping the register of nurses for their areas, approving training schools and setting examinations. When the registration of nurses commenced in 1921, qualified nurses had to pay to be included on the register which was published annually from 1922. After the Second World War it was published quarterly. Existing nurses were required to register by 1923 and until 1943 only nurses who had completed a recognised course of training could be included. The Nurses' Act 1943 made registration a legal requirement.

There are various reasons why you may be unable to locate a nurse as you research:

- the nurse could have used a second name or a nickname
- the name was indexed incorrectly on the register
- the nurse could have been a State Enrolled nurse or a Queen's Nursing Institute nurse
- compulsory registration wasn't fully enforced so many nurses didn't register
- if the nurse only worked in wartime, then she may be registered with organisations including the Red Cross, Queen Alexandra's Imperial Military Nursing Service or Royal Naval Nursing Service or the Territorial Force Nursing Service.

There are several other research resources including:

- The National Archives for military nursing records
- Royal British Nurses' Association 1887–1966 giving information on around 10,000 nurses held at King's College London Archive but available online as transcripts
- Scarlet Finders for researching nurses during World War One
- The Red Cross online for records of anyone serving in the Voluntary Aid Detachments.

Hospitals and colleges are gradually digitising their nursing records so an online search is worth doing to see which records are available. This is an ongoing project and some records may not be available because of privacy legislation.

The Royal College of Nursing archive also has around 600 recordings of individuals from the nursing profession whose oral histories provide an insight into their experiences of how nursing practice has changed and how their careers were affected by the social, political, and health changes. Your ancestor could be one of those who contributed.

In 1930 county councils took over the responsibility for workhouse infirmaries from the Poor Law Union Boards of Guardians and the Metropolitan Asylums Board. After 1948 most administration became the responsibility of the National Health Service but teaching hospitals in some locations still had their own Boards of Governors. County councils also became responsible for district nursing.

Directories and journals

Besides the official registers there are also a couple of short-lived professional directories which may provide information. The directories were published between 1894 and 1899. It was not compulsory to be listed and there was a cost for anyone to be included. The directory entries include names, addresses and brief resumes. There is also a list of training schools. The directory was known as *Burdett's Official Nursing Directory*.

Another directory – *Burdett's Hospital and Charities Annual* – also contained information but only for senior nurses as it was mainly a list of hospitals and other institutions in which nurses were employed. However, it provided some statistics on number of nurses employed at each establishment. Originally published as *Burdett's Hospital Annual* from 1890 to 1893, it assumed its longer title in 1894 and was published through to 1930. Both are available at the Wellcome library.

The *Nursing Record* was published from 1888 but became the *British Nursing Journal* in 1902. Both have been digitised and are available for research on the Royal College of Nursing Archives' website. These journals can provide valuable information including appointments and retirements, marriages and obituaries as well as giving an insight into working conditions at the time and information about salaries and pensions.

District nurses

Nursing was not restricted to just hospitals or similar large institutions. People living in rural areas also needed care. The seeds of this idea came from William Rathbone and Florence Nightingale.

Queen's Nursing Institute

This is the oldest professional nursing organisation in England and Wales and it was established in 1887 as a result of a women's fundraising initiative at the time of Queen Victoria's Golden Jubilee. Two years later in 1889, a Royal Charter granted charitable status to The Queen Victoria Jubilee Institute for Nurses. Its objectives included providing the *training, support, maintenance of women to act as nurses for the sick poor, and the establishment of a home or homes for nurses and generally the promotion and provision of improved means of nursing the sick poor.* The primary role of the institute was co-ordinating standards of district nurse training and organisation. The institute also provided trained nurses for rural work known as *village nurses* who were only employed in a district with a population of less than 3,000 and were unable to afford a fully qualified Queen's Nurse.

The institute was originally based at St Katherine's Hospital which was established as a hospital at the time of Edward III. The Metropolitan and National Nursing Association and the Rural District Nursing Association both already existed at the time but then became part of the new institution. The Metropolitan and National Nursing Association, established in 1876, was adopted as the central training home and district nurses' associations could apply to become affiliates of the institute.

There were Conditions of Affiliation for all district nursing associations. District nurses had to train at an approved hospital or infirmary and in district nursing. Training of district nurses included subjects more appropriate to home health care and included sanitation, health education, ventilation, diet, the care of new born babies and how to deal with infectious diseases.

The village nurses in country districts were required to have completed three months' training in midwifery as well as hospital service. Since inception and until the mid-twentieth century, district nurses were usually unmarried women. Nurses in large towns resided in dedicated homes and all nursing was carried out under the direction of a medical practitioner. Any interference with the religious opinions of patients or their families by the nurses was not allowed.

Nurses' homes were usually converted houses and so varied in size according to number of nurses that needed to be accommodated. In the major cities, these were often large buildings, but in rural areas they were often just small cottages. In the interwar years modern bespoke nurses' homes began to be constructed. Before the NHS was established, local district nursing associations were responsible for employing district nurses, building homes for them and paying salaries and expenses. Most associations were integrated into the Queen's Nursing Institute.

Provident schemes were established by many of the associations enabling people to subscribe so that when the need arose, they could receive nursing care. Most working-men's wages meant that private nursing was beyond the means of most families. The provident system enabled subscribers to benefit from the services of a district nurse. The National Insurance Act in 1911 changed the situation but it did not allow for free universal health care so provident schemes remained popular.

After the NHS was established in 1948, home nursing was essentially free although the changes meant that local district nursing associations ceased to exist, but the Queen's Nursing Institute continued to train district nurses until the late 1960s.

The Wellcome Library holds the national roll of the Queen's Nursing Institute from 1891 to 1969 with badge registers between 1907 and 1945 for good service. These are indexed. The Queen's Nursing Institute Roll of Nurses for the UK and Ireland 1891–1931 can also be searched on Ancestry. Other associated records useful in genealogical research are held at the Wellcome Library.

A list of the records from the Queen's Nursing Institute and the Queen's Nursing Institute Roll of Nurses can be seen at appendix 5. Other records at the Queen's Nursing Institute headquarters in London may provide more information about a district nurse including photographs, instruments used, books, pamphlets and other historical materials.

The district nursing system was organised in local/regional associations so any available surviving records will likely be available in local archives. Amongst the pre-WWI records held are:

- Trumpington and Grantchester District Nursing Association
- Wetheral District Nursing Association
- Nailsworth District Nursing Association
- Chester District Nursing Association
- Camberwell District Nursing Association
- Ribblesdale District Nursing Association.
- Liverpool District Nursing Association
- Lewes District Nursing Association.

There are many other associations whose records should cover the early-mid twentieth century.

Midwives

Midwives have practised for centuries but in the early days there were many who were not qualified and who inadvertently transmitted diseases between patients as well as causing the death of mothers and children. In 1511 an ecclesiastical licensing system for midwives came into existence, primarily so that a midwife could baptise newborn children who were unlikely to survive, thus enabling them to have a Christian burial. Licences were issued by the bishop of a diocese or from the archbishops allowing them to operate within their provincial jurisdictions.

In order to obtain a licence, a midwife was required to submit a nomination signed by her local minister and a churchwarden. From 1603 a midwife also had to confirm that she was of the Protestant faith and that she had gained experience by being apprenticed to an experienced midwife. The registers of midwives often included testimonials from other midwives or the mothers of children the licence-holder had successfully delivered.

This licensing system was suspended during the Commonwealth period 1649–1661. Ecclesiastical licensing of midwives ended during the eighteenth century and at the same time male midwives were becoming more commonplace. There were various manuals on midwifery available, many written in Latin, although some were translated and printed in English. The first manual written by a midwife, for midwives, was published in 1671.

The midwife's duties did not end with the birth of a child. If death seemed imminent, she performed the baptism ceremony. If the mother died during labour without delivering the child, it was the midwife's responsibility to open the body (perform a caesarean section) and if the baby was alive to immediately baptise it to prevent the child being "unholy" and buried in non-consecrated ground. If mother and baby survived the birth, then after the lying-in period, the midwife usually accompanied the mother to her *churching* and the second part of the Christening ceremony, accepting the child into the church.

In the early 1800s midwifery was considered a woman's job. There had been several male midwives practicing in the 1700s largely with middle and upper classes. Male midwives frequently recorded recipes for medications and tinctures. Manuals were written by doctors who exhibited specialist knowledge on childbirth although they had little hands-on experience or knowledge of the actual birthing process. Childbirth conducted in the presence of a male midwife was conducted in a way which completely maintained the modesty of the mother.

From around 1720 if a problem was envisaged or encountered during child-birth, a male midwife was able to perform delivery using forceps. Some children delivered by this process were found to be dead at birth. The male midwife was often treated with some hostility by his female counterparts. Surgeons had often refused to attend problem childbirths because they feared being blamed for deaths of children. However, legislation was passed requiring only qualified surgeons to use surgical instruments during an obstructed labour.

The Royal College of Midwifery – originally the Matrons' Aid Society later known as Midwives' Registration Society – was not established until 1881. Initially formal qualifications were not essential although many held a diploma from the London Obstetrical Society. A register of midwives examined by the society is available at The National Archives covering the period

1872–1888, but because of the poor condition of the document, research may be under supervision or the document could be withdrawn at short notice for conservation purposes.

A central board to regulate the profession was established with the passing of the Midwives' Act 1902 after which it was illegal for any unqualified person in England or Wales to practise as a midwife. After 1921 midwives had to qualify as nurses prior to becoming midwives. The Royal College of Midwives received its Royal Charter in 1947.

The improvement in midwifery services was a slow process but changes occurred as a result of the 1902 Act which established the Central Midwives Board. During the early twentieth century, the Midwives' Institute provided education opportunities as well as maintaining an employment register for the benefit of the public who were seeking trained care. The Midwives' Act of 1936 transferred the administration of midwifery services to local authorities. The Royal College of Midwives became the main provider of training courses in clinical practice.

The Royal College of Midwives administrative records include:

- council and committee minutes, agendas and reports
- departmental records
- photographs and printed material relating to the activities of prominent individuals involved in the Royal College of Midwives
- registration, training and education of midwives, maternity services, pregnancy, childbirth, contraception and abortion, dating from 1881 to the present day.

The Central Midwives' Board became the custodian of the Midwives' Roll, to prohibit unqualified and unregistered women from practising midwifery.

Midwives' roll
The Midwives' Roll 1902–1959 can be viewed digitally on Ancestry and entries include name and address, date of enrolment as a midwife and their qualification.

The originals are held by The National Archives in series DV7 covering 1883 –1983. Printed copies of the Roll are also available at the Wellcome Library; the Royal College of Midwives holds records for 1937 and 1946, and the Royal College of Nursing holds records for the period 1917–1968.

A midwife could be certified under the 1902 Act provided that she held a certificate in midwifery from the London Obstetrical Society or other certificates approved by the Central Midwives' Board, or when the Act was passed had been in legitimate practice as a midwife for at least one year and was of good character. In 1983 the Central Midwives' Board ceased to exist.

There are very few sources available for tracing midwives prior to 1902. *Nursing Notes and Midwives' Chronicle* from 1887 was the recognised monthly journal and included the names of holders of the midwifery diploma issued by the obstetric societies.

Parish registers may show some information about midwives who under-took the private baptism or recorded the burials of infants who were not baptised. These can be found at local or county record offices.

Other informative resources are the case registers, diaries, notebooks and certificates often found among personal papers of midwives. These provide an insight into childbirth and the role of midwives over time in a particular locality. The case registers may be subject to access and privacy restrictions. The Royal College of Obstetricians and Gynaecologists holds an index of registers deposited with the archives of the Royal College of Midwives. There may well be other case registers held by county record offices or even in private hands.

CHAPTER 3

THE HOSPITAL SYSTEM

Overview

The history of hospitals is immense and indeed many books have been published dedicated to this subject alone, however, what follows is a brief introduction as to how hospitals became established. Caring for the sick began in Roman and Greek times; temples in Greece were used to care for ill people, Roman soldiers wounded in battle were looked after in separate buildings and early Christian hospitals were set up in the Byzantine era.

In the mid-1300s, hospitals were usually attached and part of the local monastery which also had a chapel within their complex. Accommodation was often crowded but generally comfortable. The hospitals provided beds, food, drink, rest and treated patients with a variety of herbal remedies. The emphasis in healing patients was to do so spiritually by praying for the soul and for a speedy recovery. By 1350 hospitals became the territory of the poor because wealthier people were visited and treated by doctors in their home. St Bartholomew's, St Thomas' and St Mary of Bethlehem hospitals were the only three major medieval hospitals that existed after the dissolution of the monasteries.

The voluntary hospital movement

The voluntary hospital movement started in the early eighteenth century as charities began to look after the sick poor. It was soon recognised that the responsibility of charities to help the sick poor helped prevent destitution.

Hospitals were run by Boards of Governors made up of the local gentry and many such establishments originated as dispensaries which provided basic care when patients did not require hospitalisation or could not afford private medical treatment.

Voluntary hospitals normally depended on finance raised through annual subscriptions. Regular subscribers were encouraged although many voluntary hospitals also had to run appeals for donations.

By 1750 hospitals were also being run by councils and charities, mainly financed by the local population or through donations from benefactors. Throughout the 1700s around fifty-five new hospitals were funded in this manner.

In medieval times, only about ten per cent of medieval hospitals actually catered for the sick; people suffering from leprosy, contagious diseases, madness, pregnant women or anyone of dubious character were commonly rejected. Nearly all voluntary hospitals looked after the poor but they continued to refuse to admit people with contagious illnesses or long-term medical problems. Wealthy people continued to receive home visits.

Staffing in the hospitals consisted of nurses, physicians and surgeons. Nursing sisters treated patients with nursing helpers undertaking most of the manual work. Patients were kept warm, clean and well-nourished and were normally given herbal remedies or bled. Basic surgery was also carried out in some establishments including setting of fractured limbs and amputations.

Monastic and medieval hospitals

In medieval England, the *lepre, blynde, dumbe, deaff,* the *natural fool, creple, lame* and *lunatick* were present in everyday life. Some people were born with a disability whilst others became disabled as a result of disease or a lifetime of back-breaking work. Attitudes to disability were mixed with many people considering it a direct punishment for sin; others thought it was astrological having being born under the influence of the planet Saturn. On the other hand some were convinced that disabled people were closer to God by suffering purgatory on earth rather than after death and therefore they would get to heaven sooner. There was no overall state provision for the disabled so most lived and worked in their own communities, supported by family or friends. If they were unable to work, their town or village authorities might have supported them although many had to resort to begging. In caring for these people, the monks and nuns would follow the principal of *seven comfortable works:*

- feeding the hungry
- giving drink to the thirsty
- shelter to strangers
- housing the poor
- clothing the naked
- visiting the sick
- burying the dead.

These spiritual works also included counsel and comfort for the sick.

Many monasteries had hospitals attached to them because some of the monks had basic medical knowledge and so they were viewed as those best qualified to help the poorer community and those unable to afford the services of a physician. Clearly the church played a major role in patient care in the Middle Ages – the pinnacle of its belief was that it was a Christian's duty to care for the sick. Besides providing hospital care, the church also helped fund the ancient universities that trained doctors.

The people of medieval towns and cities and their religious institutions were actually innovators in terms of providing a specific response to disability. Their early approach to situations was the forerunner of our modern care system. It was perhaps due to the disabling consequences of leprosy which was most visible in all communities, irrespective of social class, so much so that its impact changed the mindset of its people for the better.

Leprosy, known today as Hansen's disease, was a regular feature of life by around 1050. It frequently caused gangrene, blindness, ulcerations and general debility in the skeletal frame including the loss of fingers and toes. In leper hospitals the emphasis was on cleanliness and wholesome food;

clothes were washed twice a week and their varied diet consisted of fresh food supplied from their own farms. Leper patients actually worked in the monastery farms and this had a therapeutic effect and gave them a purpose in life, enabling them to participate in their upkeep.

Leper houses were also established by the monasteries, staffed and managed by the monks and nuns. In some areas the landed gentry also founded and administered hospitals inspired by their implied Christian obligation to care for the sick. Such hospitals were established purely because of the financial support given by titled gentry, merchants or even royalty, but after the dissolution of the monasteries, the former monastery to which the hospitals were attached, would normally remain with the owners and administrators of the foundations. Funding for maintaining hospitals usually came from the community and was raised from almsgiving which at the time was considered a sacred moral duty.

At the height of the medieval period there were about 1,200 monastic hospitals most of which were associated with the church. The earliest hospital devoted to healing sick paupers is reckoned to be the Priory of St Mary of Bethlehem founded in 1247 at Bishopgate and known as the Bethlehem Hospital (later known locally as Bedlam!). During its early history the hospital began to accept patients who were suffering from mental disorders rather than physical disability or disease. The residents of Stone House at Charing Cross were transferred there in the 1370s and by 1403 the so-called 'lunatic' patients formed the majority of patients making it the most infamous, mental institution in the country. The majority of its early patients were poor and marginalised and lacked friends or family to support them.

These early institutions were managed by monks or nuns; medical care by physicians or doctors was rare. There were a few references relating to such provision at some London hospitals but in 1524 the Savoy Hospital employed both a doctor and surgeon.

Only a small percentage of medieval hospitals cared for the sick and they were only termed hospitals because they provided a place to rest and recuperate, hence "hospitality". Most were really almshouses which only provided basic nursing care without any form of medical treatment for the elderly and infirm. Other hospitals were established as hostels for pilgrims extending the "hospitality" aspect. Because most hospitals were located within monasteries, the patients or inmates effectively lived the same lifestyle as the monks and nuns. While any illness was treated in the best way possible, it was the care of the soul that was considered of primary importance. Prayer and piety were believed to facilitate the best chance of healing. Until they recovered or died, residents abided by canonical princi-ples attending daily mass, eating communally, spending time in both work and prayer, observing silence and devoting their lives to God.

In the 1530s, Henry VIII ordered the dissolution all monasteries and this had an intense impact on the hospitals because the monasteries had been the chief providers of such facilities. In the City of London the corporation petitioned the monarchy to keep the city's hospitals open. Endowments were subsequently provided for the running of some of the larger hospitals, such as St Bartholomew's and St Thomas'.

Monastic hospitals often hired local workers to look after the grounds and buildings, as well as cater for the needs of the patients; they employed cooks, laundresses and those who served as stewards and proctors and this meant that the local population had a vested interest in their monastic hospital.

The major emphasis remained the care of the poor. Poverty frequently occurred because of a physical handicap or old age. Medieval hospitals pro-vided necessary communal living. The complex was originally a courtyard layout with a gatehouse giving access to a quadrangle; this space provided an enclosed sheltered area so inmates would be undisturbed and could easily echo normal family life.

Those with other disabilities generally lived within their communities; those who could work did so, and those unable to do so were supported by their family and the local communities. Where they did not receive such support, they relied to a great extent on charity and were considered either impotent beggars or sturdy vagabonds who had to resort to begging.

Interestingly a permit was required for begging and these were strictly controlled by the authorities even to the extent that the City of London attempted, unsuccessfully, to impose a blanket ban on lepers entering the city in 1367.

Almshouses

Almshouses originated in medieval times and were originally called *bede* houses. The oldest almshouse foundation is thought to be St Oswald's in Worcester founded around 990 created by Oswald, the then Bishop of Worcester.

After the dissolution of the monasteries, it was during the late sixteenth century that the medieval craft guilds founded almshouses to provide for their *elderly decaying* members in their declining years. Many City of London Livery Companies still retain their individual almshouses. Many such schemes were supported by benefactors including royalty, senior clergy, the aristocracy, merchants and liverymen.

During the late Georgian and Victorian era almshouses became more urban in character. Housing was a huge social problem because many people from rural areas migrated to towns looking for work. Appalling conditions in the workhouses inspired wealthy philanthropists to endow almshouses, generally for their workers, and these were arranged in small groups of between six or twelve units. Around thirty per cent of today's almshouses were established during this time. Almshouses are considered to be the oldest form of social housing in Britain. One of the most famous almshouses is the Royal Hospital Chelsea, commissioned by Charles II and opened in 1692 to look after army veterans.

Founders of the almshouses often established criteria relating to who could be admitted as well as determining the governance on which it would be run. Residents were generally retired and unable to afford rent, be of good character and living in the local area. Many had to be former employees or previously followed a specific trade. Some almshouses were single sex and others accommodated both men and women, but usually in separate areas; some establishments were specifically for married couples. Almshouses were often governed by volunteer trustees and had a resident steward responsible for the day-to-day running of the unit. For many people, almshouses were a welcome alternative to other institutions such as the workhouse. Almshouse residents were seen as deserving poor and as well as providing a roof over their heads, they received a weekly living allowance.

Almshouses at Woburn, Bedfordshire

Early almshouse residents were often referred to as *bedesmen* although by the nineteenth century they were inevitably known as inmates but this was strictly incorrect. Each resident usually lived in a one-roomed house which had simple furniture and a fireplace that was also used for cooking. Some residents supplemented their allowance by taking on minor domestic duties within the complex. Many almshouses provided new clothing periodically which was worn by inmates on special occasions and when going to church. Most residents also had to abide by a strict set of rules or they could be evicted.

Unfortunately there are not many personal records of almshouse residents but some local archives might have records of charitable institutions that owned almshouses and so might have names of occupants. Residents will also appear in census records but their accuracy cannot be guaranteed because the information required was often compiled by a representative of the residents and given directly to the enumerator. Information is more prolific where the residents are tenants of a livery company or parish charity.

Depending upon the rules and conditions, some elderly people were evicted from almshouses through no fault of their own. It was quite common for a wife to be evicted when her husband died. Residents were required to live independently as the almshouses were unable to provide care for residents if they fell ill or became incapacitated. It was not unusual for almshouse residents to end their lives in the workhouse infirmary. However, by the late nineteenth century some almshouse complexes employed a resident care nurse.

Medieval hospital administration and financing
In most cases the medieval hospitals were run by a few monks and nuns in the monastery. One monk was assigned as the *proctor* responsible for collecting alms. Most of the hospitals were totally dependent on charity, although some received regular income from their patrons and some owned land or property from which they received a rental income. Hospitals also raised money by holding annual fairs under the terms of their charter and other hospitals had the right to levy tolls on local produce. Some hospitals derived a significant income from the rents received from land the monasteries owned and from benefactors' bequests. It is shown that these sources of income diminished during the period of the Black Death, a disease which also increased the number of patients thus causing additional financial difficulties.

The hospital rules governing the conduct of both patients and staff were quite strict. The master or warden was required to hold regular meetings to deal with contraventions and administer suitable punishments to those who flouted the rules. Punishments included fines, a restrictive diet of bread and water, fasting or in severe contraventions, a person may have been whipped. Food in the hospitals was normally plain and meat was served at least three times a week. On non-meat days the diet would have included dairy produce and fresh vegetables.

Early hospital beds consisted of straw pallets, but these were eventually replaced by wooden bedsteads. Sometimes a bed accommodated more than one patient. Bed linen was washed infrequently but each new patient was given clean sheets on admission.

A major factor which contributed to the decline of monastic hospitals was mismanagement. In 1414 Parliament took action to try and reduce the deterioration by passing an Act covering the reformation of hospitals. The Act was introduced because many hospitals were crumbling, both structurally and financially, but the Act had little effect. Following the Wars of the Roses, Tudor prosperity enabled new hospitals to be established replacing many of those which had existed solely through acts of religious charity.

Hospitals were not located in all areas of the country; provision may have been non-existent in one county but much better in the adjoining county. This situation was particularly true with regard to leper hospitals. The decision of who entered the hospitals rested with the patron to the extent that some prospective patients would have sought help from influential local backers to cover their entrance fee.

Medieval hospital records

Unfortunately there are few records in medieval hospitals relating to patients and staff but some information is available from the surviving monastic *cartularies* and bishops' registers, usually held by local record offices. Some established hospitals such as St Bartholomew's in London have extensive archives, in this case dating from the early 1100s and including records of staff, patients, buildings and management of the hospital and charities.

Monastic cartularies

A cartulary is basically a medieval register of lands and property. They generally included information of what lands and property were held by an abbey, monastery or nunnery, usually granted by a charter. If you are lucky, some might include names of benefactors.

Bishops' registers

Surviving bishops' registers start in the thirteenth century and in some cases the hospital's own records survive from the medieval period. Some records have been published by local record societies.

The bishops' register recorded day-to-day papal business such as:

- organisation of clergy benefices
- grants of indulgences to those who contributed to the upkeep, rebuilding or repair of ecclesiastical buildings including the medieval hospitals and information about the collections for the same purpose
- consecration of new churches or chapels, or rededication after building work
- licences issued for chapels or oratories
- papal letters.

The registers may contain information about patient admissions but that was not their prime purpose. Licences for the chapels or oratories can also be found in the Calendar of Entries in the Papal Registers relating to Great Britain and Ireland.

Hospitals in the Georgian period

The major growth and expansion of the voluntary hospitals took place in the Georgian and Regency periods – 1714 to 1837. There were around 250 hospitals established in the late 1700s, again mainly for the treatment of the poor; they existed because, as towns expanded during the Industrial Revolution, there were inadequate medical facilities and so the need for hospitals became urgent. Most were funded by subscription or voluntary donations; hence their name and they later became the general hospitals of the Victorian period.

One of the major voluntary hospitals in the country was the Royal London Hospital. Construction began in 1752 and it partially opened in 1757. Its original intention was to treat the sick poor from among the merchant seaman and manufacturing classes of the East End of London. The hospital operated on a voluntary basis where patients were not charged for treatment and their care was funded charitably from annual subscription fees.

The London Hospital, Whitechapel.

Hospitals in the Victorian period

In the early years of the Victorian era, hospitals earned the reputation of being *gateways of death* rather than *places of healing;* this was because wards were overcrowded, surgery without anaesthetic took place in non-sterile locations and there was a general lack of basic medical hygiene. Successful surgical procedures were few and far between and there was definitely a high risk of spreading disease rather than curing infections within the hospital environment.

The early Victorian hospitals had small rooms off a main corridor to try and restrict the spread of infection but this had little effect because wards were still overcrowded. It was not until Florence Nightingale influenced the design of hospitals by suggesting they included open balconies and airy wards in the hope of counteracting hospital-generated foul smells and "bad air" that conditions began to improve. After Joseph Lister discovered antiseptics and the General Medical Council began to register qualified doctors, the situation improved even further.

There were a number of different types of hospitals at this time; voluntary hospitals continued as before but there were also many new types of hospitals established – specialist hospitals, cottage hospitals, poor law infirmaries, isolation hospitals for diseased patients and asylums for the insane.

Throughout the nineteenth century, the government took more responsibility for the provision of health care. As well as workhouse infirmaries for the destitute, local authorities began to establish hospitals for the general public. Medical and nursing staff, as opposed to charitable donors, began to play a more prominent role in hospital administration. By the 1890s Britain had a good system of hospitals and poor law infirmaries catering for most social classes. Each type of hospital embodied a different type of medical need. This hospital system existed up to the establishment of the National Health Service in 1948.

By the end of the nineteenth century, industrialisation, urban migration and overcrowding put tremendous pressure on all hospital services. In many of the larger industrial areas, workers contributed to local medical charities as a type of health insurance. The majority of unemployed, chronically sick or seriously ill patients who could not afford the voluntary hospital fees ended up with medical care provided by poor law infirmaries.

The number of hospital beds tripled between 1861 and the end of the nineteenth century. By 1926 local government had taken over administration of poor law infirmaries, metropolitan hospitals and asylums.

General hospitals

General hospitals, some of which remained voluntary, were for those who could not afford to pay for hospital treatment. These hospitals normally denied admission to anyone who had sufficient financial means to pay for their treatment, those who should be in the asylum system or victims of highly infectious diseases. General hospitals were public institutions for administering medical and surgical relief to inpatients as well as those attending as outpatients who were suffering from general illness or disease.

People with incurable or contagious diseases were referred to the special hospitals.

Many general hospitals were initially established in larger private houses where big rooms were converted into small wards, a board room and a chapel facility. As the movement expanded so did purpose-built premises, assuming the governors could raise sufficient funds. By using purpose-built premises, common standards existed for ventilation and sanitation. Many also had separate buildings housing the kitchen, other domestic offices and a mortuary.

In the eighteenth century various medical societies supported research into new scientific methods and many new hospitals were opened. The Industrial Revolution created great wealth so rich businessmen began to donate money so that new voluntary hospitals could be opened to accommodate the growing population. It is known that eleven such hospitals were opened in London with a further fifty throughout the country. Hospitals also evolved to become training centres for both for doctors and surgeons. Treatment remained free. The eighteenth century also saw the establishment of public dispensaries.

By the mid-nineteenth century, new model hospitals followed the 'pavilion' system in which ward blocks, known as pavilions or Nightingale wards, were all connected to a central administration block with sanitary facilities in annexes. There were variations of the pavilion plan. Nurses' living accommodation was also incorporated in hospital sites.

Most of patients who were admitted to general hospitals suffered from acute diseases but patients suffering from cancer or other incurable disorders were not usually admitted. Surgical operations were generally rare before the introduction of anaesthetics in the late 1840s. The introduction of antiseptics and anaesthetics improved surgical treatment. Hospitals that had started training centres then began to establish medical colleges, ultimately becoming teaching hospitals and centres for medical research.

General hospitals normally depended upon either voluntary or local government contributions and were under the management of a board of governors, who qualified as such because of a financial donation or annual subscription. Medical treatment was usually managed by non-resident physicians and surgeons, not in private practice, selected by the governors. The doctors were supported by a paid apothecary. Each physician or surgeon looked after his own patients and attended only on specific days. They were assisted by the resident medical officers who were responsible for daily routine treatments. Other doctors who were working in the hospitals received their income from fees charged to their private patients not from the hospital funds.

Patients were admitted on specific days by recommendation of a governor or doctor unless emergency treatment was needed. In some of the larger hospitals sickness alone, without recommendation, was sufficient to claim admission. Some hospitals had a medical school attached specifically for the training medical students; the lecturers and instructors were usually the medical officers of the hospital and the fees paid by students were often the only means of income that these officers received.

General hospitals for foreign nationals
In the port cities and in London particularly, hospitals were established specifically for the treatment of poor foreigners; the first one was the French Protestant Hospital established by the Huguenots in the first decade of the eighteenth century. A German and Italian hospital followed as did various Jewish ones, mainly within London's East End. In such establishments, nursing care for those who were terminally ill began to be provided by the Catholic convents.

The French Hospital was established as an almshouse in Finsbury in 1718 for the benefit of poor French Protestants and their descendants who resided in Great Britain. It was among the earliest foundations to improve the welfare of needy immigrants and was believed to be the first in Britain to provide care for the mentally ill.

From around 1720 the hospital was known as *La Providence;* initially it had eighty beds but by the 1760s it was catering for around 235 patients. By the 1850s the hospital was in urgent need of repair so the governors decided that it would be more economic to move elsewhere. Thus in 1862, three acres of land in south Hackney were purchased and a brand new hospital was built and opened in 1865. It accommodated forty women and twenty men and was staffed by a steward with nurses and servants. The building also included day rooms, library and a chapel. The records of the French Protestant Hospital (*La Providence*) and its subsidiary charities are held by the Huguenot Library for the period 1718 to the present day.

Cottage hospitals

As previously mentioned, although voluntary hospitals could trace their origins back to the medieval period, it was really in the mid-eighteenth century that these establishments expanded. The voluntary hospitals were centres of acute medicine, providing care for patients with specific diseases; with their expansion came the establishment of cottage hospitals.

Cottage Hospital, Welwyn, Herts. Typical small cottage hospital built to serve communities

The original concept of a cottage hospital was a small rural building with just a few beds; the advantage of providing this type of care avoided patients having to take long journeys to county or voluntary hospitals for treatment. Cottage hospitals were also able to deal more immediately with emergencies. The other advantage was the fact that patients were dealt with by the local doctors who were aware of their circumstances. Local knowledge about a patient might have got lost had they been referred to another hospital.

Between 1855 and 1898, nearly 300 cottage hospitals were established but as early as 1818 a village surgeon in Southam in Warwickshire opened a cottage hospital with just four beds; it was specifically for manual labourers and their families. Then in 1827 cottages at Piccotts End near, Hemel Hempstead became the first real cottage hospital which provided free medical services. The cottage hospital system was really got underway and expanded in the 1860s.

Most cottage hospitals existed for the immediate treatment of local patients who would otherwise have to visit the nearest larger hospital. Cottage hospitals were very popular amongst both urban and rural communities in the 1860s. They varied in size, depending upon the community they served, but most of them had a small dispensary and a small operating theatre; they normally only admitted patients with minor ailments and did not cater for various categories of patients, including epileptics, the chronically ill, or maternity cases.

The hospitals did not have the monopoly on care as local government and the poor law authorities also provided similar hospital facilities. For poorer members of any community who needed long-term care because of illness or old age, the poor law workhouse infirmaries were often their final retreat. By the end of the nineteenth century and into the early 1900s, most areas of Britain had a rather fragmented hospital provision – some were private hospitals which charged fees, some were charity voluntary hospitals and others had been established by local authorities. Something needed to be done.

The National Insurance Scheme in 1911

The beginnings of the modern welfare state really started with when the government passed the National Insurance Act 1911. This momentous piece of legislation paved the way and gradually changed the situation with relation to the provision of medical care nationally.

In simple terms, monetary contributions were made by workers and employers, and the government then promised money to double the value of their contributions thus providing workers with free medical care and sickness benefits. No new system works smoothly straight away and this system was no exception as it did have some shortcomings:

- it only covered some occupations
- it did not include the dependents of those covered
- it did not it cover the elderly or those with long-term conditions.

In 1920 cover was extended to workers earning up to £250 a year unless they were agricultural labourers or domestic servants – and families were still not included. This then created a problem because during the 1930s, many people living in the more deprived areas of the country found that the quality of healthcare had deteriorated. People were unable to afford medical care.

The reforms of the health system from the 1930s into the early 1940s resulted in the gradual demise of the cottage hospitals – as contributory schemes such as national and private insurance raised demand for hospital services, so the charity donations on which voluntary hospitals had relied started to decline. However, having said that, some cottage hospitals continued to thrive after the introduction of the National Health Service in 1948.

The nation was at a turning point having come through the First World War followed by a general strike. The Second World War resulted in greater government control showing that a unified service could work efficiently – thus the NHS was formed and ultimately took voluntary hospitals into public ownership funded by taxation and staffed by salaried professionals.

The idea and dream of an all-encompassing medical treatment system was gaining momentum.

Specialist hospitals

The first specialist hospital was thought to be the London Lock Hospital established in 1786 for treating patients with sexually-transmitted diseases. Most patients suffering from venereal disease were excluded from the voluntary and general hospitals because they were deemed to have sinned.

Throughout the nineteenth century specialist hospitals evolved from the previously established dispensaries. Most were located in London and the major cities and concentrated on the treatment of eyes, ear, nose and throat, skin, orthopaedics and vital organs. By 1870 there were around seventy specialist hospitals in the London area, however, many were forced to close as the larger teaching hospitals began to establish specialist departments.

Specialist hospitals were for patients who suffered from a specific condition or medical need, and one that a particular doctor wanted to treat. The specialist hospitals only allowed patients to be admitted by the doctors working at the hospitals. These doctors normally permitted entry based on the conditions of the patients and how they wanted to treat that condition; this system allowed doctors to further their research. Some of the specialist hospitals were funded by relatives of those who had been treated in them as well as by the doctors who had an interest in the illness or disease itself.

One particular hospital of note was Moorfields Eye Hospital, established in 1805 as the London Dispensary for the Relief of the Poor Afflicted with Eye Disease. At the beginning of the nineteenth century, ophthalmology was an unknown science. Up until then, the treatment for eye disease was the domain of itinerant quacks. Moorfields treated soldiers returning from serving in India and Egypt through the Port of London and who were afflicted by eye diseases which would otherwise have spread thus rapidly infecting others.

The first hospital specifically to treat women existed from the mid-1840s and by 1870 there were twelve similar establishments throughout England.

The most well-known was the Elizabeth Garrett Anderson Hospital in London, named after the first woman doctor. Although they were run on the same basis as general hospitals, they only admitted women and young children because they specialized mainly in gynaecological problems. General hospitals also began to set up their own specialist gynaecological departments.

The Hospital for Sick Children in Great Ormond Street opened in 1852 with only ten beds and two physicians but within the next twenty years nearly forty specialist children's hospitals existed throughout England and Wales. Prior to the NHS in 1948, Great Ormond Street was a voluntary hospital, running fundraising campaigns for new buildings from the 1850s onwards.

The Royal Marsden Hospital specialising in cancer care opened in 1852 but there was little that could be done to treat the disease until X-rays and radium treatments were developed towards the end of the century; this was quickly followed by the pioneering surgical removal of tumours and chemotherapy.

The *British Medical Journal* actually ran a campaign against specialist hospitals as it believed doctors were being taken away from the basic philosophy that a doctor should be competent in every aspect of medicine and they argued that there was no room for those specialising or concentrating on one small aspect of medicine. This ultimately proved futile and not for the benefit of patients.

Isolation Hospitals

To prevent the spread of infectious diseases, isolating the patient was considered essential and there was generally free treatment to encourage patients to enter these hospitals and protect the public from exposure. In 1802 the first isolation hospital for smallpox and infectious diseases was opened and became known as the London Fever Hospital. Many such establishments followed during the nineteenth century but it wasn't until the Isolation Hospitals Act in 1893 that county councils were able to establish provincial isolation hospitals. These municipal isolation hospitals were generally large with rows of detached ward blocks.

The Smallpox Hospital, Highgate, Middlesex.

The Industrial Revolution brought many social changes and the population grew with people living in small, overcrowded houses, on cramped streets and with elementary sanitary arrangements; this in turn created a massive increase in sicknesses and diseases which the authorities struggled to control. Still believing that infection was carried in *miasmas* (transmitted by unhealthy smells and air), doctors established isolation hospitals to stop disease from spreading. At the hospitals there were separate blocks or wards for each disease and strict hygiene rules were applied to prevent patients being infected by other illnesses.

The development of antibiotics and vaccinations dramatically reduced the incidences of these infectious diseases thus leading to the demise of many of these hospitals just after the Second World War. Many of them were converted into sanatoriums or care homes for elderly patients.

Subscription hospitals and funding

Subscription hospitals were not always the same as the general and voluntary hospitals previously referred to although there was an element of subscription towards their funding. At the start of the eighteenth century, limited hospital facilities expanded with the advent of the subscription hospitals within London and in certain areas outside the capital. While subscriptions remained the main source of funding for these hospitals, the Saturday Fund set up in the 1850s collected weekly contributions from workers' wages and this scheme existed into the early twentieth century.

Patients could only avail themselves of subscription hospital facilities if they obtained a letter of recommendation from a hospital subscriber which had to state that they were a *proper object of the charity*. Most people also had to pay a deposit towards the cost of a burial should they die whilst in the hospital. Some hospitals also required patients to obtain a letter from the authorities confirming that all funeral expenses would be met by the parish or poor law union.

Public dispensaries complemented the subscription hospitals as these offered alternative means of obtaining medical treatment and drugs. These were also financed by voluntary contributions which enabled patients to be treated without cost by retained doctors with an apothecary available to dispense medicines. The Saturday Fund where money was collected on payday was supplemented by the Sunday Fund which boosted funding from the church collections.

Workhouse and poor law infirmaries

Organised welfare provision in different forms had existed in Britain from the time of Elizabeth I. After the dissolution of the monasteries, the responsibility of looking after the poor gradually passed to government. Since the Poor Relief Act 1601, parishioners paid the poor rate, based on the value of their property and the money collected was then distributed to those in need by the elected ecclesiastical parish overseers. The poor rate also funded medical care for the sick but help was only given to paupers who had legal settlement within the parish.

Most parishes and the Gilbert Union workhouses that existed in the mid-eighteenth to early nineteenth centuries were too small to house an infirmary ward but after 1834 infirmaries were usually annexed to all union workhouse plans.

Private workhouses known as metropolitan pauper farms were established in the early eighteenth century. Large numbers of paupers in London, particularly those who were incapable of work because of insanity, imbecility or feckless personality, or who were difficult to manage in ordinary parish workhouses, were placed in these pauper farms. In the eighteenth and early nineteenth centuries, these pauper farms formed an important part of public welfare provision. After the Poor Law Amendment Act of 1834 and the Lunatics Act of 1845, their role was largely incorporated into the union workhouses and the county lunatic asylums.

Medical treatment within the workhouse infirmary system clearly left much to be desired, even after the establishment of the union workhouse. Nearly every union workhouse provided at least a small infirmary to care for sick inmates. Early nursing care was usually carried out by the competent female inmates rather than paid nursing staff or medical attendants.

Initially the poor law infirmaries were established within the workhouse system solely for the inmates of that workhouse. The infirmaries were required to accept everyone whereas voluntary hospitals could choose their patients. Originally, the infirmaries occupied rooms within workhouses where patients received very basic care, although admission to an infirmary carried a similar social stigma to that of entering the union workhouse. Doctors who were working in the infirmaries were only paid for their time, but because of the poor conditions, some doctors didn't want to be involved. The infirmaries gained a reputation for being some of the worst institutions of the Victorian era and this made recruitment of doctors difficult. By 1867 some union infirmaries were removed from the workhouse environment to separate buildings, usually purpose-built; this was prompted by deaths of inmates due to neglect and following pressure from the medical profession about poor care standards although remaining under the control of the Board of Guardians.

The infirmaries could accommodate a number of chronically ill patients who were mainly the aged and infirm. Many also had substantial maternity facilities although birth certificates for those born in infirmaries tended to use the street address as opposed to indicating a birth within a union workhouse or infirmary.

Amongst the authorities it was generally felt that health care could be more cost-effective if provided by an organisation with fewer but better equipped institutions, so the government introduced a new bill which was specific to London and aimed to improve the management of the sick and other poor in the city. The Metropolitan Poor Act 1867 meant that the unions and parishes covering London became part of the Metropolitan Asylums District managed by the Metropolitan Asylums Board. The board's initial responsibility was to provide specialised accommodation for fever and smallpox patients, certain types of mental cases, and sick children with long-term ailments or those convalescing.

London was divided into Sick Asylum Districts:

- Poplar and Stepney
- Kensington
- Finsbury
- Central London
- Rotherhithe
- Newington.

The board also established the training ship system in 1875 which pro-vided naval training to pauper boys up to the age of sixteen, as well as establishing children's hospitals for those suffering from eye, skin and scalp diseases, those who were deemed educationally sub-normal and those who required long-term nursing or convalescent care. The board also developed smallpox and fever hospitals, smallpox hospital ships, the River Ambulance Service and tuberculosis sanatoria. As a result of the efforts of the Metropolitan Poor Act, more infirmaries were built nationwide. Further detailed information about the training ships moored on the river and also the River Ambulance Service can be found in appendix 6.

Workhouse Visiting Society

The Workhouse Visiting Society, established in 1858, exposed poor standards of nursing care in the infirmaries and recommended that the treatment of sick inmates should be under the general management of a matron who had previous hospital training. Qualified nurses, many of whom were "Nightingales", took charge of nursing with menial duties undertaken by suitable female pauper inmates working under qualified supervision. The first twelve nurses to be trained at the Nightingale Nursing School were employed in a Liverpool Infirmary in 1865. Despite recommendations of the Visiting Societies it was not until 1863 that infirmaries employed qualified nurses.

Increases in the number of beds in the infirmaries did not always mean an increase in the quality care. The *Lancet* ran a campaign in the 1860s to raise awareness about the poor conditions in workhouse infirmaries and subsequently standards began to improve. In 1869 it was estimated that around 50,000 thousand sick paupers were inmates of union workhouses or their infirmaries.

Responsibility for administration of the poor law passed to the Local Government Board in 1871 and the emphasis moved towards the care of the sick and helpless paupers. The Diseases Prevention Act 1883 allowed workhouse infirmaries to offer treatment to non-resident paupers as well as inmates and by the beginning of the twentieth century some infirmaries began to operate as private hospitals.

From the 1880s admission to workhouse infirmaries was offered to those who, although from the poorer classes, were not sufficiently destitute that they needed to enter the workhouse to be afforded the facilities of the infirmary. The admission of non-paupers to the infirmaries led to the physical expansion of facilities and the increase in staffing levels. During the First World War many were used as military convalescent hospitals and afterwards never reverted to infirmary status.

Public dispensaries

In 1687 the College of Physicians announced that its members would, in certain circumstances, provide free treatment and medicines to the poor, so it opened a public dispensary at the college in 1698. There was opposition to the scheme from some members but this was the beginning of many such establishments.

However, it was not until around 1770 that dispensaries were established in significant numbers. Most of these dispensaries were funded by voluntary subscriptions with the subscribers recommending the people who received treatment. Medical practitioners at the dispensaries offered their services for free.

The public dispensaries provided outpatient medical treatment and advice while serving to compliment the inpatient services provided by hospitals. The services were provided exclusively for the sick poor. In some dispensaries home visits were also available. The Dispensary for the Infant Poor established in London in 1769 was short-lived because its focus on infant poor only was too small and specific.

Two dispensaries were set up by the Methodists. John Wesley worked in medicine which was an important feature of his movement and he was instrumental in opening the first free medical dispensaries. The early Methodists showed a profound concern for the care and the medical welfare of the poorer members of the community. In an attempt to overcome the healthcare differences between the social classes of the eighteenth century, Wesley opened his first free medical dispensary in London in 1746. Prior to this he had already set up a scheme for the care of the sick in many Methodist societies. The success of the London dispensary inspired Wesley to start medical ministries in other areas including Newcastle and Bristol and his dispensaries were the first of their kind in England.

Wesley worked in the dispensary in London and prescribed many of the medications himself although he worked alongside both an apothecary and a surgeon. Wesley also knew that the costs associated with treatments at hospitals made healthcare unaffordable for the poor. He estimated that in the first few months of its opening, over 500 poor people were prescribed medicine at the London dispensary many of whom were not Methodists.

John Wesley's vocation was to serve the poor; he had a fascination with medicine which encouraged him to become a skilled amateur physician. He promoted self-help by establishing free health care. He recorded clinical information including signs and symptoms and potential diagnoses and treatments in his diaries and journals. Despite this he often visited physicians with his own illnesses and encouraged others to do likewise. He often discussed medical practice with an uncle who practised as a London doctor.

Wesley became convinced that many doctors were putting financial gain above patient welfare. He considered that many prescriptions generated by such professionals were expensive and complicated, so much so, that he publicly attacked those who did so as unethical. He openly accused the profession of raising their status by being too technical and by using both astronomy and astrology to deliberately mislead or confuse people. He was also suspicious of doctors who prescribed compound drugs.

In 1747 Wesley published a self-help manual entitled *Primitive Physic* to provide trustworthy advice for his followers; it was in the format of a basic medical handbook for the home. The paper-bound publication originally cost one shilling and became one of the most popular books of its time. *Primitive Physic* advocated fresh air, cleanliness and readily digestible food; he also advised readers not to use specifically potential toxic substances such as opium that were in common usage and recommended by contemporary medical books. The book effectively made Wesley one of the greatest health educators and his book was widely believed to have been the most popular medical book of its time.

The collection of remedies provided in the book were not devised by Wesley but were arranged alphabetically according to symptoms or illnesses dealing with everything from baldness to cancer as well as discussing many everyday disorders such as asthma, gout, diabetes, and sciatica. He encouraged his readers to use readily available herbs, flowers and household products in their treatments and did so by including recipes for medicines that could be produced at home.

Public Dispensaries were essential as they carried out treatment that hospitals did not want to undertake. The relationship between dispensaries and the hospitals was complex. Various groups of people were excluded from hospitals – pregnant women, sufferers of sexually transmitted disease, those with contagious diseases and even children. This is why the dispensary provision was essential; many founders of the dispensaries were themselves members of the excluded groups because of religion or nationality.

Public dispensaries were gradually replaced with Provident Dispensaries which worked on a subscription basis offering medical care to people who made a small weekly subscription which was normally one penny per week. By 1800 both types of dispensaries dealt with at around 10,000 admissions in any one year. One of the earliest provident dispensaries opened in 1830 in Coventry. Subscriptions were one penny a week for adults and a half-penny a week for children.

This type of scheme allowed working-class people to be self-reliant, therefore avoiding charitable treatment given to paupers. In order to function properly, the provident dispensary needed a few hundred members in order to finance the services of one doctor. Some of the dispensaries also benefitted from philanthropic investment and some arranged for hospital specialists to see dispensary patients at reduced fees. Doctors at some provident dispensaries also undertook home visits.

Other public dispensaries were established in the following areas:

London
The Foundry, Moorfields, was opened by Methodist preacher John Wesley in 1746

- Finsbury Dispensary, London, founded 1780
- St. Mary's Dispensary for Women, London, founded 1866
- Surrey Dispensary, founded 1777
- Warwick Lane dispensary, London 1688–1725

- St. Martin's Lane dispensary
- General Dispensary, Aldersgate Street.

Elsewhere in Britain
- Ardwick and Ancoats Dispensary, Manchester, founded 1828
- Edinburgh Provident Dispensary for Women and Children founded 1878
- Public Dispensary of Edinburgh founded 1776.

Convalescent hospitals

There were once many convalescent homes throughout Britain, particularly in coastal resorts and in rural areas. A period of convalescence was an important part of the patient recovery process. In the nineteenth century, patients who were discharged after having undergone surgery or who were recovering from an illness were often re-admitted to hospital because of a relapse, mainly attributed to not being able to convalesce properly at home. Living conditions meant that many returned to work before they had fully recuperated and likewise wives and mothers had to look after the children and resume housework. From the mid-nineteenth century hospitals started to establish convalescent homes.

It was soon recognised that full recovery could not take place within a hospital environment or within the patients' own homes. Convalescent hospitals helped solve the problem; it meant that patients could be discharged more quickly from hospitals and be able to recover in a homely rather than institutional environment where food was better and they could still obtain proper rest and care.

Florence Nightingale was again influential in the establishment of convalescent hospitals advocating that every hospital should provide such facilities. Her objective was that patients should not stay in bed but use the facilities provided which included common rooms, day rooms, libraries, billiard rooms, entertainment rooms and above all gardens where they could relax. The hospitals were also to be built either at seaside resorts or within a country setting.

Initially patients were cared for in wards but as their recovery progressed they would be transferred to smaller rooms to become a little more independent before being discharged when they were fully recovered. Many Victorian hospitals sent their patients on discharge to convalescent homes for further recuperation before allowing them home. Some convalescent homes were maintained by contributory schemes where small subscriptions were made from wages meaning that workers contributed towards their health care.

Dreadnaught Seamen's Hospital Greenwich

The Dreadnought Seamen's Hospital at Greenwich was the main hospital providing relief to sick and injured seamen from around the world. Men returning home after the Napoleonic Wars ended continued to suffer from illness and disease which had resulted from their service; their afflictions included scurvy, smallpox, cholera and sexually-transmitted diseases. In 1817–1818 a public subscription fund known as The Seamen's Hospital Society was created specifically for the relief of suffering mariners so the idea of a dedicated hospital for seamen was born with the objective of treating them and to help them find employment on other ships once discharged.

Between 1821 and 1870, the hospital was based on three successive converted warships. The first was HMS *Grampus* loaned by the Admiralty and moored at Greenwich. The first patients were admitted in October 1821. By 1831 HMS *Grampus* was not large enough and was replaced by HMS *Dreadnought* which served 250 patients and a further 150 in convalescence. Eventually HMS *Dreadnought* also became too small and was replaced by HMS *Caledonia* although the name *Dreadnought* continued to be used, courtesy of the Admiralty. As it was a floating hospital, it was still at risk from infectious diseases so alternative land-based accommodation was developed in the infirmary block of the Royal Hospital Greenwich which had become vacant in 1869 after Royal Navy inpatients were no longer admitted. The Admiralty leased the building to the Seamen's Hospital Society for the treatment of merchant seamen.

In April 1870 patients were moved into the new building and the Dreadnought Seamen's Hospital was dedicated to the treatment of civilian mariners. The Dreadnought Medical Training School was established seven years later with two dispensaries added in 1880. The hospital became the centre for tropical disease research.

When the Dreadnought hospital closed, the original registers were deposited with the National Maritime Museum. They provide:

- admission data
- brief medical details including medical condition, illness or injuries
- how patients were discharged.

Casualties including women and children were sometimes admitted as a result of local emergencies. Wounded servicemen were admitted during the First World War. The 1918 register volume includes information on members of the Royal Naval Division wounded in the trenches of the western front.

The admission registers have significant research value to family historians because they provide a snapshot of the health of maritime personnel from all nations for over 150 years and document the risks to health at sea and how medical treatments advanced as they applied at maritime life.

The admission registers, some of which are available on Ancestry include:

- hospital number, date of entry, name and place of birth
- quality or rank and age
- ward or where placed in hospital
- ship's name and port
- nature of complaint and number of days in hospital
- nature of departure – discharge date or death date.

The London Metropolitan Archives hold mainly administrative and management records for the Dreadnought Seamen's Hospital including:

- papers of the Medical Council
- Staff Consultative Committee minutes
- nursing subcommittee minutes
- medical staff committee minutes
- registers of death and operations.

General administrative papers between 1900 and 1939 are held at the Wellcome Library.

Epilepsy colonies

Like many afflictions during the Victorian era, epilepsy was not fully understood so sufferers were often stigmatised. Employment prospects for sufferers were virtually non-existent with many ending up in workhouses or even county asylums through no fault of their own. The National Society for the Employment of Epileptics purchased a farm at Chalfont St Peter in Buckinghamshire in 1893 and this establishment provided both nursing and medical care together with employment for epileptic sufferers from all over the country.

In 1894 the first male sufferers were admitted, each being charged ten shillings a week. If they could not afford to pay, then funding was available to cover the costs. The staff at the time consisted of a lady superintendent, a bailiff, a male attendant, a nurse and a female servant. Only sufferers with *reasonable behaviour and mental ability* were admitted to the colony.

They worked on the land or undertook domestic work around the home for six days a week. The men were also involved in such practical trades as carpentry, plumbing, painting and bricklaying. The philosophy adopted by the establishment was that fresh air and hard work was beneficial to health and well-being as opposed to reliance only on drugs. The farm was visited by medical staff from the National Hospital for the Paralysed and Epileptics based in London.

By 1900 the colony had expanded to accommodate around ninety men and forty women who were strictly segregated because colony patients were not allowed to marry. In 1909 after a school was built, children were also admitted. As well as receiving an education, the children also worked for about twelve hours a week. Scout troops and guide companies were also formed and there were various social activities, treats and outings organised for the children.

Homes for inebriates

Drunkenness for many was a normal part of everyday life but after the Industrial Revolution and certainly by the early years of the Victorian era, there was an increased need for a sober, punctual and reliable workforce which prompted a change to people's lifestyle and attitude. The Temperance and Band of Hope movements grew principally because the problems associated with urbanisation were largely blamed on alcohol abuse.

There were both men and women who were chronically addicted and regarded as inebriates whose alcoholism inevitably led to an early death. Beer sold to the working classes was often adulterated with strychnine which was used to mimic the bitterness normally associated with hops. In 1788 Thomas Trotter, a Scottish physician, suggested that chronic drunkenness was a disease after which *delirium tremens* brought about by the withdrawal of alcohol, was first noted in 1813.

A subsequent campaign by medical professionals resulted in treatment for inebriates, the philosophy being that they could be treated successfully if they were removed from their addiction source and were subjected to enforced abstinence. In 1870 there was an attempt by Parliament to introduce legislation which would forcibly confine habitual drunkards in reformatories so that they could receive the necessary medical care and moral guidance. However, that bill was defeated because habitual drunkards were considered to be *a minor social problem*. Strong opposition was also expressed by brewers and those involved in the drinks trade so the bill was defeated.

In 1872 a House of Commons Select Committee on Habitual Drunkenness was established and it recommended that a Drunkards' Register be kept and that two types of infirmaries be established – one for those able to pay for the compulsory treatment as convicted drunkards and one for those who could not afford to pay. This resulted in three homes for inebriates in Bakewell in Derbyshire, Sheerness in Kent and one for females in Edinburgh. Treatment was both medical, using mustard plasters to *draw out the poisons,* and spiritual. Most of the patients stayed for about three or four months. None of these homes appeared to cater for the working classes.

Legislation was finally enacted in 1879 lasting initially for ten years in order to advance the care of habitual drunkards who were not certified as lunatics, but who were a danger to themselves and incapable of managing their own affairs. By 1888 the definition of habitual drunkard changed to inebriate. This Act did not satisfy campaigners because they wanted compulsory detention for all habitual drunkards. Unless criminal acts had occurred or the drunkard was declared insane, other inebriates were able, without any fear of consequences, to continue to live in their communities although they inevitably passed the addiction to younger family members.

The Inebriates Act of 1898 paved the way for non-criminal inebriates to be admitted to institutions for a maximum of three years – but only if they had been convicted four times in one year for drunkenness. By the start of the twentieth century, there were still only fifteen licensed inebriate institutions which peaked in the years leading up to the outbreak of the First World War. After the end of the war, prosecutions for drunkenness fell because of reduced opening hours of public houses and the general reduction in the strength of alcoholic beverages.

Patient admission to hospitals

Before the NHS was established in 1948, admission to hospitals was not an automatic right. Admission was either through:

- nomination by a governor or subscriber
- because of a petition
- the payment of fees
- the provision of a surety to guarantee payment of burial expenses should a patient die.

Fees were usually paid by relatives, friends or by the patient's residential parish authorities. Occasionally hospitals waived fees for cases of extreme need. Sureties, where required, were from the patient's own parish, their employers or a military or naval officer if the patients were wounded soldiers or sailors needing treatment.

Medical care was sometimes reduced because of an incorrect diagnoses based on limitations through lack of understanding about the human body or unproven medical theories. Surgery was rarely carried out because of the lack of anaesthesia. Most hospitals only offered patients a bed and food together with basic medicines and external cures.

Conditions inside most hospitals at that time were unhygienic; bed bugs were common! Contagious diseases including typhus could also spread easily amongst inpatients. Notwithstanding these factors the death rate amongst patients was relatively low because most were treated and discharged as quickly as possible.

Some patients refused to comply with hospital regulations so they could have been prematurely discharged for disruptive behaviour. Patients also frequently lied about their personal circumstances and medical conditions in order to gain admission and then discharged themselves when they felt they had received sufficient treatment. Some poorer people became experts at manipulating the system in order to secure the care they needed.

Towards the end of the nineteenth century, changing attitudes and the role hospitals played in medical education altered the relationship between doctors and patients. Doctors and surgeons began to exclude the patient from their diagnostic deliberations, whereas before patients were very much involved in the decisions made. It is possible that this change in attitude was in response to the increasing demands poor patients placed on doctors. However, the result was to sideline patients in the provision of their medical care.

Despite this hospitals provided an important service to the community which had previously been unavailable to the majority. Together with the introduction of dispensaries, hospital care contributed significantly to the improvement in living standards and decrease in death rates.

Life on the wards
Most general hospitals served the working industrious poor and specialist hospitals became extremely popular with the middle classes who could

afford to pay. These charges remained less than the private medical treatment afforded by the upper classes.

Inpatients

As most early general hospitals operated a subscription system, wealthy members of the community paid annually which allowed them to nominate both inpatients and outpatients for treatment, hence only those with such a recommendation received treatment.

Those needing treatment could appeal to a subscriber in their community for a recommendation, known as a *ticket* and mostly obtained from the local clergy, board of guardians or a recognised doctor. Some larger employers including railway companies were subscribers which enabled their employees to receive treatment when needed, provided they could satisfy certain conditions and be deemed suitable cases.

Inpatients had treatment restricted to a maximum period of six weeks, known as *standard time*. Armed with the ticket, patients were granted admission and had to attend on a specific day. The ticket also detailed any items that the patient was required to take into a hospital. Strict hospital rules applied to every patient irrespective of status and anyone disobeying the rules could be immediately discharged. The rules related to order and discipline on the wards including not smoking, swearing, drinking or gambling, none of which were conducive to the best treatment that the hospitals provided.

It was not unusual for patients to pawn possessions including the tools of their trade in order to pay towards their treatment. Many hospitals had a *Samaritan Fund* where donations or subscriptions raised enough money to help impoverished patients to re-equip themselves and continue to earn a living once discharged. Donation boxes were placed in outpatient departments where patients who could afford to do so could contribute.

Outpatients

Most Victorian outpatient departments were the early accident and emergency departments because those attending would receive essential treatment and then be sent home. The overcrowded waiting halls were a breeding ground for contagious diseases and infection; they were frequently policed by porters who regularly evicted patients, particularly if they were under the influence of alcohol. Outpatients could receive medicines, crutches, spectacles, and other surgical appliances. Trusses for hernias were regularly given out in areas where patients worked in heavy industrial labouring jobs.

Victorian operating theatres

Anyone needing to undergo surgery in the 1860s was making a life or death decision. Developments in anaesthesia prevented agonising and painful experiences but post-operative infections, gangrene and septicaemia still affected a high proportion of surgical patients. In the early Victorian period, the way to try to prevent infection and disease spreading was to ventilate all the hospital wards to remove the miasma which doctors then believed was emitted by wounds.

Victorian operating theatre

It was quite normal for surgeons entering the operating theatre to be wearing their everyday street clothes; without washing their hands, they donned their surgical gowns which had not been washed or sterilised and were often covered in dried blood and body fluids from previous operations.

During surgery the surgeons hung suture threads from their gown eyelets to keep them handy for use. Surgical instruments were normally cleaned once the operation was concluded but not before the next use. If any instruments fell on the ground, surgeons just picked them up, wiped them on their gowns and carried on using them. In rural areas, it was not unusual to apply a cow-dung poultice to the wound at the end of the operation. In the recovery room nurses would use the same instruments on different patients.

The operating theatres had tiered wooden observation galleries from where medical students would watch the operations, hence the origin of operating *theatre*. Students crowded into the galleried rows and some were even within touching distance of the patient or the surgeon. All observers wore their street clothes – no gowns or masks at all. The importance of the operation and the reputation of the surgeon influenced the number of spectators.

The wooden operating table resembled a carpenter's bench and was located in the centre of the theatre. Surgery was performed using basic anaesthesia or antiseptics and sometimes without either. Often the students and sometimes surgeons were overcome by the ether in the atmosphere which was being used as the anaesthetic and which filled the room. When amputations took place, sawdust was spread beneath the operating table to soak up the blood. Patients were also known to wake up from their opiate-induced stupor during the operation. It was not unusual for patients to be blindfolded whilst on the operating table so they would not be able to see the procedure. The chances of death from the effects of an operation were high because of the shock and trauma, loss of blood, or post-operative infection. Most operations only lasted a short time and amputations by a skilled surgeon could be completed in less than five minutes with additional post-operative time allowed for stopping blood flow and dressing the wound.

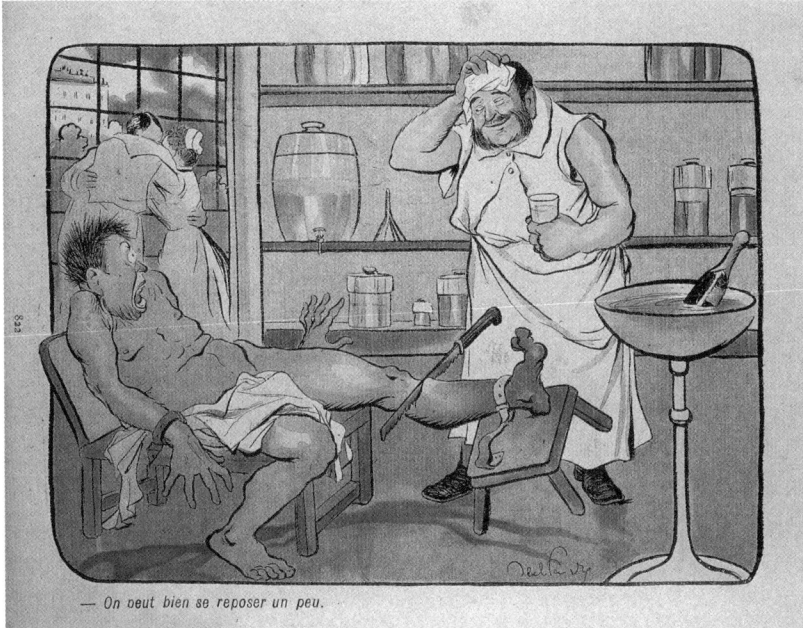

— On peut bien se reposer un peu.

A surgeon apologetically takes a breather during an amputation operation: a bottle of champagne waits in a cooler; a doctor and nurse canoodle while the patient screams.

If any of your ancestors underwent amputation surgery, then the surgeon would have followed a procedure similar to the following:

- Patients laid on an operating table were told to keep very still. A slight movement compromised the operation and could have fatal results.
- Tourniquets using canvas straps were placed above the incision to stem the flow of blood, tightened using a screw attached to brass plates on either side.
- Surgeon's instruments resembled large curved bladed knives to make the incision through flesh and muscles surrounding the bone on each side of the limb.

- The surgeon then cut completely through the bone with an amputation saw. The dismembered limb dropped into a bucket of sawdust under the operating table to absorb the blood. The student observers then applauded the surgeon's work.
- Once the limb was free, the surgeon would seal off the main artery and smaller blood vessels, and when and if the blood stopped flowing, he would stitch up the wound.
- The stump would be bandaged.
- At the end of the procedure the patient was taken away for recovery.

Around one third of amputees did not survive because hospital conditions of poor sanitation and hygiene often resulted in deadly infections, not because the surgery was unsuccessful.

Hospital records

Hospital records are an underused resource for family history – but they do exist. As medicine became more specialised in the later part of the nineteenth century and early twentieth century, patients often travelled out of their own locality to receive treatment from particular physicians or surgeons.

Because of administrative mergers, the archives of many hospitals may now be in one central place; some hospitals also have their own archives. Patients' case notes were first kept as teaching aids in the mid to late nineteenth century. Part of the research challenge is that the survival of case records may be selective and only kept where cases were unusual or interesting.

However, hospital records can be a goldmine of information for tracing both staff and patients. We can learn about medical advances and the records give an insight into the attitudes of our ancestors towards disease and death from both the medical professional and the patient perspectives. The survival rate of records is spasmodic because many were discarded and others may still be subject to privacy closure periods. If you are lucky your ancestors may have been treated in a hospital which still exists today and which may have its own archive department. Some hospitals have deposited their records with county record offices. The Hospital Records Database is a good place to start. In 1957 hospital records were declared public records. (See website listing.)

Hospital and doctors' patient records

The most useful record to start with is your ancestor's death certificate. Death certificates can tell us about any ailments that our ancestor suffered as well as giving the cause of death. Certificates often indicate how long the deceased had suffered from a particular illness. Cause of death is important even if it only states *natural causes* or *old age*. In the early Victorian period before the many medical science advances, the recorded cause of death may not always have been accurate. Some of the causes may be described using unfamiliar terms. For example, anthrax was often recorded as *wool-sorters' disease* but that may provide additional clues about someone's occupation or environment. There are various lists of obsolete or archaic medical terms and causes of death available on the internet.

Starting your search using a death certificate often leads to many different questions and curiosities. Doctors' records are often a key resource because most doctors kept meticulous records of their patients' treatment. However, before Victorian medical advances, doctors had their own ideas of diagnosis and what patients were suffering from. Patients' records compiled by doctors outside the hospital system relate to all social classes. Many of our ancestors would have suffered from the effects of epidemics such as flu, smallpox or cholera and many lost their lives as a result.

Records of general practitioners, where they survive, are normally accessible in local archives. They can include records of vaccinations given to family members, drugs and potions prescribed. Doctors were paid a fee by the parish overseers to administer smallpox vaccinations to all the families within a parish. From the records of individual doctors and from general records of a village or town community, you may be able to link epidemics, particularly if there were a large number of deaths recorded in the parish burials registers within a few days of each other. Occasionally gravestones show the cause of death, particularly where the tragedy was as a result of an unusual act or epidemic.

Understanding patient records is probably another challenge because you will need to read the doctor's handwriting. However, they will nearly always be illuminating in content. If an ancestor was a patient within the workhouse infirmary, then patient records may be few and far between; often the only records that exist are those of the general workhouse such as admission and discharge registers although there may be separate lists for the infirmary.

Hospital records database

This database is invaluable to locate records of many hospitals. There is currently information on just under 3,000 hospitals around the country. Information was originally compiled by the Wellcome Library. The database was last updated in 2012 and is no longer being updated, so do be aware that information such as the location of records may be out of date. It is important to supplement the database search by using The National Archives' Discovery catalogue to find other records held at either TNA or in other repositories, even if they are listed on the hospital records database. If you know the location of the hospital in question, it is also beneficial to consult the local record office catalogue for similar information.

Information shown in the hospital records database includes:

- hospital administrative records
- clinical records
- staff and personnel records.

Some hospital records will be subject to closure periods. Access is not generally available for patient records less than 100 years old, although there are exceptions, most of which require a doctor's intervention. It does mean that records before 1924 are unrestricted but it is still advisable to check with the repository as some record volumes may include information from a later date.

There is also a more specialist but important database providing statistical information about voluntary hospitals. It is the Voluntary Hospitals Database, provided by the London School of Hygiene and Tropical

Medicine and covers voluntary hospitals in Britain and Ireland between the 1890s and 1940s.

Even after reviewing the database you could find that records are incomplete as they had an uncertain future once the clinical and administrative periods had ended. There was also inadequate funding for the maintenance of a hospital archive so patient and staff records may well have been destroyed after a relatively short time.

Staff records

Hospitals were staffed by many people so personnel records are important. If your ancestor was an administrator, nurse, student or orderly, then records may well exist. However, you are unlikely to be able to find a personnel file, so delving into administrative records and even researching outside the hospital records will be needed. You may need to look at minute books or financial ledgers to glean information. Administrative records could also include information on appointments and promotions of staff and may include CVs or details of an ancestor's employment conditions. Some hospitals kept intricate records on their nurses' recruitment and of their medical students so you can track progress of your ancestors prior to qualification. The website Scarletfinders is excellent if your ancestor was a military medic. See website listing for details.

Staff magazines and journals can be invaluable, particularly for obituaries of staff although these seem to relate to more senior staff; nevertheless, they will provide a good potted history of your ancestors' medical career. Medical student records maintained by the larger teaching hospitals will show:

- enrolment
- who their mentor was
- address
- details of any degree or apprenticeship
- curriculum timetables of study
- which ward rounds they were on
- lectures they attended.

Other medical school records may survive showing fees paid by students, prizes awarded, handbooks etc. all providing an insight into your ancestors' lives.

Patient records

The most prolific sets of records for patients are the hospital admission, discharge and death registers. As the records are normally chronological, you need to have a good idea of when your ancestor was a patient or when they died. You may find that some registers are indexed otherwise researching particularly in the larger hospital records can be time-consuming.

Information in the registers should contain:

- name, address and age
- date of admission, discharge or death
- ward admitted to and consultant's name (sometimes)
- general remarks

Where a death is recorded, additional information including results of any post-mortem and the cause of death will normally be given and some may include the name of the next of kin and undertaker. Hospitals usually kept separate post-mortem books which, although full of medical jargon, can provide a valuable insight into what caused the death.

In a similar vein most hospitals kept operating theatre registers which show details of surgical procedures. Again most will be chronological. Patient case notes were originally kept by doctors for their own personal use and only a small number of these early records survive. They may be amongst any surviving personal papers of the doctor. Where they exist, they are normally intricate in detail and provide a portrait of a patient's time in hospital.

By the mid-nineteenth century, systems were evolving for the compiling and storage of case notes by the hospitals as opposed to the doctors personally. However, it was much later that all hospitals adopted systems for routinely keeping patient records. These case notes generally contained details of diagnosis and treatments. Where hospitals provided teaching facilities, they would keep additional records relative to research, dissection of donated bodies and other teaching processes carried out on their patients.

Children's hospital records

The Historic Hospital Admission Registers Project provides access to some 140,000 admission records from 1852 to 1921 for four children's hospitals:

- Great Ormond Street Hospital
- Evelina Children's Hospital
- Alexandra Hip Hospital for Children
- Royal Hospital for Sick Children, Glasgow.

The case notes of two eminent early paediatricians can also be accessed, as can a library of articles relating to children's health in both Victorian and Edwardian Britain. Family historians will find masses of information on families and healthcare in the Victorian and Edwardian eras.

The Great Ormond Street records are continuous for the whole period but the other hospital records are not quite as comprehensive. The Evelina records cover 1874 to 1877 and 1889 to 1902. The Alexandra Hospital for Hip Disease cover 1867 to 1895, and Glasgow hospital records cover 1883 to 1904. The individual hospitals included variable information in their registers.

The registers include some or all of the following information:

- child's name, age (in years and months), gender and address
- diagnosis, dates of admission and discharge and the outcome of treatment
- name of the admitting doctor
- the child's sponsor and the ward to which they were admitted.

The Alexandra Hospital was opened in 1867 at Bloomsbury having been founded by a group of women who wanted to help children suffering with tubercular arthritis. Two of the women were Great Ormond Street nurses who had first-hand experience of the hip disease. From 1867 to 1870 it was known as the House of Relief for Children with Chronic Diseases of the

Joints, and between 1870 and 1881 it was rebranded the Hospital for Hip Diseases in Children.

The Evelina Hospital was founded 1869 by Ferdinand de Rothschild in memory of his English wife, Evelina; she had died during childbirth in 1866 and the hospital was financed entirely from Rothschild's personal wealth. Initially he had planned a maternity hospital in Southwark but was persuaded that there was a more urgent need for a general children's hospital, specifically to accommodate poor children south of the river Thames.

Great Ormond Street Hospital began in 1852 in a converted seventeenth-century house. At this time London's population had grown extensively following the Industrial Revolution. The population expansion was not matched by growth in hospital provision and the long-established general hospitals could not cope with the increase in demand. Hospital care available to the thousands of children living in poverty in London was minimal. The healthcare that was available before Great Ormond Street Hospital opened was normally provided by the dispensaries.

The hospital was funded by subscriptions and donations. Its services were provided free of charge, exclusively for the children of the poor. Wealthy donors and patrons became governors of the hospital and were entitled to recommend a number of patients to be admitted each year, dependent upon their contribution. In the formative years of the hospital, patients were treated for a wide variety of conditions from serious illnesses such as bronchitis, phthisis and syphilis to relatively minor ailments like catarrh and diarrhoea, and this was all in shared wards. Case notes for the patients of Great Ormond Street Hospital have been digitised and part-transcribed and can be accessed on the Great Ormond Street database.

CHAPTER 4

MEDICAL ADVANCES AND PIONEERS

Every medical advance had a significant impact on the health and well-being of our ancestors. There were many medical discoveries and advances throughout the Victorian period (and some earlier) which enabled better health and lifestyle although many diseases still existed in epidemic proportions. Common diseases of the time were usually extremely dangerous or even fatal. Many children died or became seriously ill before vaccinations became commonplace. The degree to which children suffered from diseases and ailments also varied considerably.

Vaccination

It is without doubt that the discovery and implementation of vaccinations saved many lives, especially from the nineteenth century onwards. But it is also true to say that throughout the years there has been some resistance to this procedure; there are even arguments still going on today about the efficacy of the covid vaccinations. Nevertheless, it cannot be denied that some sort of control over infectious diseases had to be regarded as a good thing.

John Williamson

Most people associate Edward Jenner as the doctor who successfully tested and introduced a vaccination to eradicate smallpox. However, there was one man who worked on this same topic several years earlier in Shetland.

John Williamson (c1730-c1803) was known by his nickname *Johnnie Notions*. Like many islanders he had many occupations … it was a case of *needs must* for people living on the edge. Men and women were expected to be able to turn their hand to anything and Johnnie was no exception; he was a tailor, joiner, clock- and watch-mender, blacksmith, farmer, fisherman, weaver and self-taught physician!

Island populations are particularly prone to large-scale outbreaks of disease, especially if it is brought in by a visitor from the mainland. This was the case in the early 1700s and records show that many people in Shetland and Fair Isle lost their lives to an outbreak of smallpox. So it was that Johnnie turned his attention to the problem of smallpox. Through trial and error and rudimentary medical knowledge, he eventually developed a vaccination which in fact was highly successful; it was highly regarded by the people of Shetland as it is believed that he never lost a patient! It is thought his inoculations were done in late 1780s but many people think it was even earlier than that.

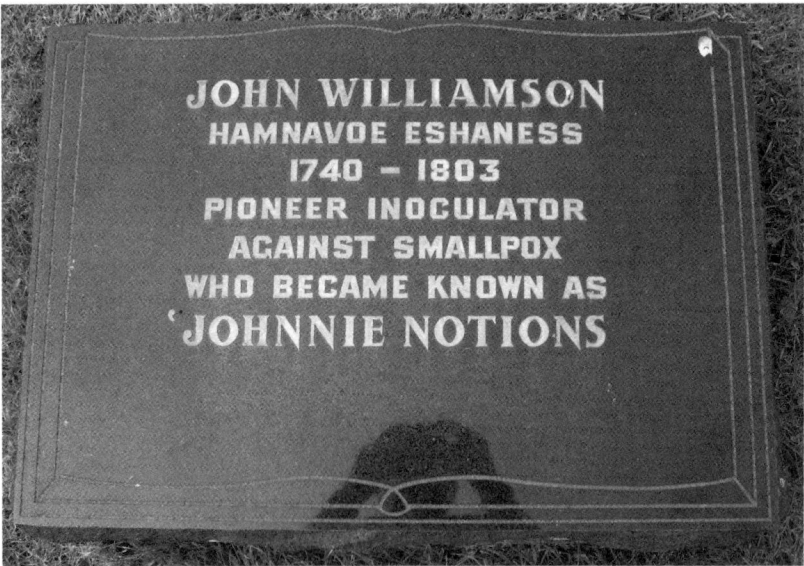

Memorial plaque to John Williamson in Shetland

Johnnie's work has been somewhat overshadowed by that of Edward Jenner, nevertheless, he is well-remembered in Shetland. His memorial stone is in the Cross Kirk cemetery, Eshaness, Shetland.

Edward Jenner

Edward Jenner was a surgeon in the late eighteenth century and he established the germ theory of disease. Smallpox was caused by a virus in the human respiratory system that developed over twelve days, after which patients had noticeable symptoms including fever, muscle aches, headaches and spots covering the face and the extremities which ultimately scabbed over permanently disfiguring their victims, assuming they survived the disease. Jenner himself suffered from smallpox and after diagnosis went through a process where he was bled and then inoculated with a live smallpox virus from which he successfully survived.

Edward Jenner

Jenner overheard a milkmaid say she would never suffer from smallpox because she had had cowpox. This gave him the idea of injecting healthy humans with the cowpox to see if it protected them from smallpox. In the spring of 1776, when an outbreak of cowpox occurred near Berkeley, Gloucestershire, Jenner extracted blood from the milkmaid who was suffering from cowpox and successfully inoculated a boy who was infected by the smallpox virus. The vaccination was successful and from then on Jenner became recognized as the pioneer of immunology.

Measles

Measles, medically known as *rubeola*, was considered by Victorians to be a mild disease, although without immunity it was a killer. The symptoms of measles appeared as a cold followed by fever and then a classic red rash developed. Many children also had other symptoms such as earache or fits. As a consequence of catching measles, other problems often manifested themselves including pulmonary consumption; thus measles was often fatal.

German measles

Known medically as *rubella*, German measles had similar symptoms to measles although swollen glands around the neck were a further telltale symptom. German measles was considered to be a mild disease too but it had consequences particularly for pregnant women because unborn children could be affected by deafness, sight impairment or heart conditions. This disease was rarely fatal, but the consequences would usually be life-changing.

Vaccination controls

Records of vaccination provide an insight into the attempts made to control diseases and can provide some valuable family history clues. Vaccination records are amongst the many underused resources for family historians. Most of the records commenced in the mid-nineteenth century when vaccination schemes became more widespread and were successful in eradicating many of the prevalent killer diseases.

Vaccination became compulsory under an Act of Parliament in 1853 and its administration was under the supervision of poor law union boards of guardians. Poor law unions were divided into districts for the purpose of vaccinations. Parents or guardians of children born after 1 August 1854 had to present their children for vaccination within three months of their birth. The local registrar kept a register of successful vaccinations; but this process was not popular and objection to the system meant that some parents deliberately avoided registering the births of their children in order to evade vaccination. This is one of the reasons why a birth certificate may not be located.

Distrust of the system gave rise to the anti-vaccination movement. Thousands of people opposed compulsory smallpox vaccinations on religious, moral and ethical grounds. A further Vaccination Act in 1867 made it a criminal offence to deny a child vaccination up to the age of fourteen.

The government's response to the 1870 smallpox epidemic was the passing of a further Vaccination Act in 1871 requiring vaccination officers to be appointed by the poor law boards of guardians to enforce vaccination of infants. Vaccination officers recorded the births and deaths of infants in the registers enabling them to monitor which infants had been vaccinated and locate those who had not. Parents who refused to have their children vaccinated could be prosecuted and this was also recorded in the vaccination registers. Any child who died before vaccination was also noted in the register.

A succession of laws made vaccination free and then compulsory. Some towns formed their own anti-vaccination leagues which later combined to form the National Anti-Vaccination League in 1896. The league continued to oppose compulsory vaccination and ended up with 103 branches around the country with a membership of around 10,000.

In June 1867 the publication *Human Nature* indicated that a number of petitions had been given to Parliament including those from parents who alleged that their children had died as a result of actually having the vaccinations. The journal reported the formation of the Anti-Compulsory Vaccination League and quoted its founder Richard Gibbs … *I believe we have hundreds of cases here, from being poisoned with vaccination, I deem incurable. One member of a family dating* [sic] *syphilitic symptoms from the time of vaccination, when all the other members of the family have been clear. We strongly advise parents to go to prison, rather than submit to have their helpless offspring inoculated with scrofula, syphilis, and mania.*

After the death of Gibbs in 1871 the league went through several changes until 1876, when it was led by the Rev. W. Hume-Rothery and his wife. It subsequently published the *National Anti-Compulsory Vaccination Reporter*. In 1880 the league was again reorganised with the formation of The London Society for the Abolition of Compulsory Vaccination; the *Vaccination Inquirer*, established 1879, became its official journal.

Vaccination lists compiled from birth registrations by the poor law union vaccination officer were organised in districts and subdistricts. Poor law unions and the civil registration districts were basically the same administrative unit.

Most vaccination registers contained The Vaccination Acts 1867 and 1871 and included the Notice of the Requirement of Vaccination. The fine for not being vaccinated within that time was twenty shillings; for many people, this was more than a week's wages. Many children were vaccinated when they were between one and two months old. A vaccination could only be postponed if the child was not medically fit to be vaccinated, the proviso being that once recovered, the child had to attend the next public vaccination clinic.

Surviving vaccination lists usually provide the following information:

- name of the child
- name of the father (or mother where the child is illegitimate or father deceased)
- date and place of birth
- father's occupation
- date of vaccination and against which disease.

Some records were not fully completed. The registers normally consisted of two parts: the return of all births registered and the register of certificates completed after a successful vaccination.

Most registers in this series are available up to about 1909 although some exist up to the start of the First World War. Later registers often contain more medical detail but do not always record the child's date and place of birth or the parents' names. The vaccination registers are available at county record offices and are a useful alternative when a child's birth registration cannot be found. Most vaccination records can be found amongst the Board of Guardians' minutes for the poor law union or in some cases are held by local authority health departments. Survival rates of the registers vary.

Some records reveal details about the prosecutions of parents; these can usually be found in the vaccination officers' report books as well as in the Quarter Sessions court minutes. The officers also communicated with each other to keep track of families who moved from one area to another. It is also worth researching the records generated by medical practitioners as these might also record vaccinations in the medical day books or patient case notes. If the child's forename was not included, their gender is nearly always shown. There are some register entries which show identical names, usually meaning that the same child attended for a second vaccination after a few months.

In 1898 Parliament passed a further Act to allow parents to opt out of the compulsory vaccination of their children by introducing a conscience clause; this entitled the parents who objected to vaccination to apply to a local magistrate for an exemption certificate. This provided poorer members of the community with relief from crippling fines and from the continued threat of imprisonment.

By the end of 1898, over 200,000 certificates of conscientious objection had been issued, mainly in areas where anti-vaccination propaganda was rife, although conscientious objection to vaccination was by no means restricted to those areas. An Act of 1907 amended the conscience clause making conscientious objector status much easier to obtain and resulting in around a quarter of children registered at birth not being vaccinated. Most of the applicants for exemption certificates were working-class people and many were women.

Louis Pasteur

In 1861 Louis Pasteur proved that bacteria caused diseases. In the nineteenth century people believed that "bad air" caused diseases and this was endorsed by the plague doctors and supposedly explained why diseases like cholera existed. It wasn't until Louis Pasteur pioneered microbiology and discovered that microorganisms were the cause of infectious diseases, not "bad air". Although Pasteur's theory was correct, many practitioners discarded the theory early on. Pasteur's theory was backed up by Robert Koch, another microbiologist who carried out his own research on bacteria which caused anthrax and he continued his research into infectious diseases by experimenting with tuberculosis.

PASTEUR DANS SON LABORATOIRE

Louis Pasteur

Pasteur recognized Edward Jenner's research and experimented in order to overcome rabies by creating a vaccine for it. Rabies was a virus that attacked the nervous system and it was normally transmitted through a bite from a rabid animal. He located a dog infected with rabies and extracted a sample from the dog's spinal cord. After two weeks, dogs were inoculated with emulsions from the spinal cord that had been dried for fourteen days. It proved to be effective in dogs and gave immunity to rabies although this did not mean humans would be immune. In 1885 Pasteur successfully treated a young boy aged eight infected with rabies.

Joseph Lister

Joseph Lister, born 1827, is recognised as the developer of antiseptics; in fact he became known as the *father of antiseptics*. Lister was a surgeon who was concerned that many patients died soon after surgery. He had learned about germs from Pasteur's works and began experimenting with chemicals in order to clean patients' wounds. He discovered that cleaning wounds and surgical instruments with antiseptics improved the survival rate of patients.

Joseph Lister's steam spray

123

High death rates from surgery gave rise to various campaigns for the practice of surgery to be stopped. Lister soaked bandages in carbolic acid to keep wounds clean. Patients' post-operative wounds began to heal properly with this treatment; he therefore concluded that a surgeon's hands, protective gowns and surgical instruments should be sterilised as well using this chemical. The successful process opened the door for many other surgical procedures because there was less likelihood of infection. Lister also developed a carbolic acid spray machine to clean operating theatres but this was not deemed to be the universal solution because breathing the fumes was dangerous. Lister's legacy was a massive reduction in the deaths of surgical patients because of infection.

John Scott Burdon-Sanderson

John Scott Burdon-Sanderson worked at St. Mary's Hospital, London and began his research into penicillin in the 1870s. He discovered that cultures covered with mould did not result in bacterial growth. Burdon-Sanderson's discovery enabled Joseph Lister to discover that urine samples contaminated with mould prevented the growth of bacteria describing the action as *penicillium glaucum*. (*Penicillium glaucum* is also a mould that is used in the making of some types of blue cheese – but that's another story!)

A nurse at King's College hospital whose wound did not respond to antiseptics was given penicillium as a cure. In 1875 John Tyndall followed up on Burdon-Sanderson's research by demonstrating to the Royal Society the antibacterial action of the penicillium fungus. The discovery of penicillin was a major medical breakthrough as it was the first effective antibiotic.

Although penicillin had now been discovered, it was Alexander Fleming who realised its importance and developed its use. During the First World War, Fleming was aware that antiseptics did not prevent infection, particularly in the deep battle wounds encountered by soldiers. So he tried to find something that would kill the bacteria that caused major infections. On returning from his holiday he found that the bacteria he had grown in some old Petri dishes were being killed by the penicillin mould. Antibiotics had effectively been discovered by accident.

Felix Hoffman

In 1897 Felix Hoffmann, a German chemist, blended acetylsalicylic acid into a stable form for medical application, marketed for the first time as aspirin in 1899. Having studied pharmacy at the University of Munich, Hoffmann was employed in pharmacies throughout Germany.

However, acetylsalicylic acid had already been discovered in England as early as 1763 when it was extracted from willow-tree bark. The use of willow bark was an established remedy for pain during medieval times when the extracts from boiling the bark were used for healing purposes. The large German pharmaceutical company, Bayer, endorsed Hoffmann as the inventor of aspirin.

Other advancements

Throughout the Victorian period the medical profession significantly improved their knowledge leading to better patient experiences and cures. Many scientific developments increased the understanding of health, hygiene and medicines amongst the general public. Many pharmacists had laboratories as part of their shops and continued to research other new and effective treatments.

In the first half of the nineteenth century medical professionals raised expectation that treatments were an exact science. Nearly 8,000 university-qualified men entered the medical profession in Great Britain to keep pace with the growth in population. Many worked in hospitals which also expanded to meet demands for treatment. In 1800 hospitals had around 3,000 patients but by 1850 patient numbers had increased to about 8,000.

Hospitals provided opportunities for the training of doctors, particularly after the Apothecaries' Act 1815, which stated that six month's experience in an infirmary, hospital, or dispensary was a requirement for qualification. The larger teaching hospitals, which became important centres for study, were inundated with medical students after the passing of the Anatomy Act of 1832. Its introduction also meant that all unclaimed deceased bodies were sent to the teaching hospitals for dissection providing a much greater opportunity for students to perfect their skills.

Inroads were also made into pharmacology. Many new drugs were invented or discovered. The nineteenth century was also a notable period for the identification and treatment of many diseases. People from all social classes keenly followed developments and ideas which gradually led to Britain becoming a much healthier nation.

Some medical instruments and techniques were also discovered or invented during the Victorian period. The benefit of all these advances to every one of our ancestors is obvious as their return to good health would have been much quicker and less painful than earlier. Death was also less likely. A short explanation of some of these advances and discoveries is found below.

Ophthalmoscope

If our ancestors suffered from any eyesight problems, then this invention would have been paramount to their treatment. The instrument was introduced in the early 1850s by Hermann von Helmholtz. It was not originally known as an ophthalmoscope but the name became common after 1854. It was used for examining the interior of the eye using a beam of light which enabled otherwise invisible tissues to be examined. Prior to its invention, little was known about the eye's composition behind the pupil. Improved machines using the same principle are in common use today.

Hypodermic syringe

Many people probably cringe at the thought of having an injection but without this invention, many medical treatments which our ancestors needed would have been impossible to perform. Prior to 1853, early vaccinations were done by inserting the vaccine into the patient by making a small cut or scratch. Well before the invention of the syringe, needles were used to extract body fluids so our ancestors may well have been familiar with the process.

In 1853 the hypodermic glass syringe evolved from work undertaken by Alexander Wood. He used the instrument initially to inject medication in the treatment of neuralgia. Because of its success, he published the findings in the *Edinburgh Medical & Surgical Journal* in 1855. Around the same time,

Charles Pravaz from Lyon in France had developed a metal syringe with a hollow needle.

Syringe technology was not new and once the hypodermic syringe existed, injections revolutionised the practice of medicine. From the 1830s physicians began to think of using syringes to inject medication. The first hollow needle for such purposes was made in 1844. From 1865, Wood's glass cylinder syringe replaced the earlier metal syringe because doctors could more easily gauge what dosage of medication to administer.

Physicians believed that injected medication only affected the area around the injection but this idea changed when injected substances were seen to generally treat pain effectively. A further development in 1899 gave the profession a patented one-handed syringe that enabled a physician to inject without assistance.

Stethoscope
The stethoscope was invented in 1816 in France primarily because doctors were not comfortable placing their ear directly onto a woman's chest to listen to her heart. It consisted of a wooden listening tube. The original device was similar to an ear trumpet. In 1840, an instrument, described as a stethoscope, had a flexible tube but the first published description of a stethoscope described it as a *snake ear trumpet* having a single earpiece. In 1852 the stethoscope that used both ears became standard and from then on revolutionised diagnosis.

Pasteurization
Louis Pasteur accidentally discovered pasteurization while trying to understand why wine and beer sometimes soured during fermentation. He performed a test which involved the gradual heating and then rapid cooling of the liquids until the offending germs were neutralized. Hence, pasteurization had been invented.

Tuberculosis was, at this point, commonly carried by milk. Pasteur patented his heating and cooling process in 1865. Machines known as milk pasteurizers were first commercially produced in 1882 and a technique known as batch pasteurization was developed.

Nearly every family in the land benefitted from this process as it had a significant impact on tuberculosis, although it did not prevent it. The pasteurization of milk became standard practice by the late 1800s. However, in many communities pasteurised milk was unavailable and did not become standard until the first decade of the twentieth century. Pasteur's discovery helped to reduce the numbers of people suffering from tuberculosis contracted by milk.

Contact lenses

In 1845, Sir John Herschel published his ideas either for a spherical capsule of glass filled with animal jelly or for a mold of the cornea that could be impressed on a transparent medium. Molds taken of living eyes enabled lenses to fit the actual shape of a person's eye.

Early contact lenses

Various developments occurred from the 1880s. In 1887 a German glassblower developed a transparent eye covering. Previously any comfortable device placed on the eye impaired vision; the earlier devices were not that comfortable. The construction and fitting of the first successful contact lens was in 1888 with the development of a focal contact shell that was designed to lie on the less sensitive area of the eye around the cornea. The perfected lenses made from blown glass were about three-quarters of an inch in diameter. The wearing of the lenses was more comfortable because the space between the cornea and lens housed a dextrose solution acting as a lubricant.

In the late 1870s German scientist August Müller produced a slightly more convenient and comfortable glass-blown contact lens. The glass-blown lenses were the only form of contact lens available until the 1930s when Plexiglas was used to make them. (Plexiglas was actually a plastic made from acrylic resin which allowed thinner and more comfortable lenses to be made.)

General anaesthetics

Laughing gas, ether and chloroform all numbed pain during surgery and their use increased throughout the Victorian period. It was in the early nineteenth century that medical professionals and scientists began to experiment with anaesthetics to put patients to sleep during painful procedures.

In 1846, American dentist William Morton claimed he was the first person to use ether as an anaesthetic when extracting a tooth, although several other dentists made similar claims. The use of ether in Victorian operating theatres became hugely popular; Robert Liston, a Scottish surgeon, was the first in Britain to amputate a limb using ether as an anaesthetic. Ether had side effects because it made patients vomit and was highly inflammable, so operating near lamps and fires was almost impossible. Although it sent patients to sleep, it could also cause long-term damage their respiratory system.

In 1847, James Simpson first used chloroform successfully when he experimented on himself and a couple of colleagues. Simpson initially used chloroform to ease labour pains during the birthing process but he soon became aware that it could become a reliable general anaesthetic. Despite objections to its use, it allowed surgeons more time to operate successfully and undertake surgery with more precision.

Some surgeons still preferred their patients to be awake during surgical procedures in order that they could monitor their survival. Unfortunately in earlier days of its usage, it was difficult to get the dosage right, so some patients regrettably died due to overdosing.

The use of chloroform as an anaesthetic resulted in what became known as the *twenty-year black period* when the death rate actually increased – surgeons took their time in operations and patients tended to overdose on the anaesthetic. In the 1850s John Snow developed an inhaler to regulate the dosage and the fact that Queen Victoria was administered chloroform during the births of two of her children made the general use of chloroform more acceptable to the public.

Nitrous oxide was discovered by Humphry Davy, a teenage chemist, in 1799. Experimenting with new gases to inhale, Davy found that nitrous oxide not only caused exhilaration but also gave significant pain relief. Davy's findings were kept largely for personal recreational use. It wasn't until much later that laughing gas was used extensively within the medical world. Nitrous oxide was amongst the first anaesthetics to be used although it was not suitable for use in long operations. Davy is also well-known as the inventor of the Davy Lamp in 1815, widely used in mines.

Local anaesthetics

A local anaesthetic prevents transmission of the nerve impulse in the region to which it is applied and does not affect consciousness. In 1860 German chemist Albert Niemann created cocaine by distilling the leaves of the coca plant – *erythroxylum coca*. Cocaine proved to have analgesic properties and in 1884 the first surgical eye operation under local anaesthesia using cocaine was carried out. As this was successful, cocaine became common-place in other surgical procedures as a local anaesthetic. However, it had many disadvantages due to its toxicity and addiction properties which proved problematic.

Although using cocaine had shown it was possible to perform an operation without causing the patient unnecessary suffering, there was a need to find something other than cocaine. An alternative appeared in 1905 in the form of novocaine which became the most-used local anaesthetic until the 1940s. It was a derivative of cocaine but it did not have the toxicity or addictive properties of cocaine. Much improved local anaesthetics became popular by the mid-twentieth century.

The X-ray

X-rays for medical purposes were discovered almost by accident in 1895 but had been around before that time as a type of unidentified radiation emitted from experimental discharge tubes. William Morgan in 1785 was reckoned to be the first person to accidentally produce X-rays. His discovery was further investigated by Humphry Davy and Michael Faraday who was at one time Morgan's assistant.

Physics professor Fernando Sanford created an *electric photograph* which generated X-rays. In 1886 he became familiar with cathode rays and in 1888, Philipp Lenard conducted experiments where he measured the penetrating power of these rays through various materials giving rise to the birth of the modern day X-ray system.

In 1895 Wilhelm Röntgen, a German scientist, stumbled on X-rays and he later wrote a paper about them. He referred to them as "X" indicating it was an unknown type of radiation. Röntgen's laboratory notes were burned after his death so there is no known surviving evidence of his research, but he was recognised as the discoverer of X-rays for medical use when he took a picture of his wife's hand. The resulting photograph stimulated interest among the scientific and medical fraternities.

The first use of X-rays under clinical conditions was undertaken in Birmingham in 1896, when an X-ray was taken of a needle stuck in a patient's hand. In that same year X-rays were first used during a surgical operation. From this time onwards, X-rays became the major diagnostic tool allowing doctors to see inside the human body without recourse to surgery. X-rays were first used on a military battlefield to locate bullets and broken bones in wounded soldiers in the war between Italy and Abyssinia, just one year after their discovery. Subsequently X-ray technology was used in several British colonial wars, the Greco-Turkish war, and the Spanish-American War in 1898.

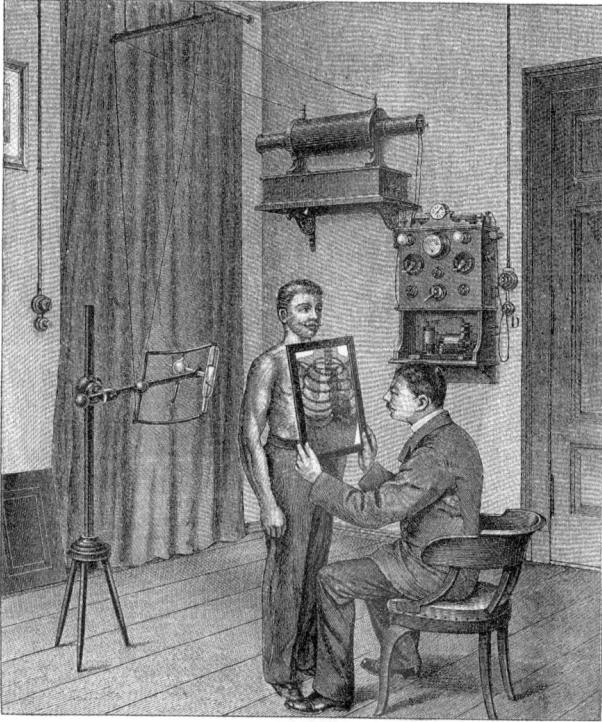

Doctor analysing an X-ray

In 1904, Clarence Dally, an assistant to Thomas Edison, worked extensively with X-rays. He died from skin cancer and his untimely death caused scientists to take the radiation risks involved with X-rays seriously, although they were not fully understood at the time.

From the 1930s to the mid-1950s retail shoe shops used fluoroscopes which used X-rays so that customers could see the bones in their feet and the shop assistant could ensure a proper fitting shoe. The practice ended when it was determined to be a health risk due to emitted radiation particularly affecting children. Some people even regarded it as a gimmick.

Marie Curie

Most people probably associate Marie Curie with the discovery of radio-isotopes, radium and polonium as well as being a hero of the First World War. Marie Curie was instrumental in taking mobile X-ray machines onto the battlefield. Her own research was put on hold when German troops headed to Paris in 1914 as a result of which she took her stocks of radium to Bordeaux to be stored hoping that once the war ended she could reclaim it and continue her research. During the ensuing war, she redirected her scientific skills to saving soldiers' lives.

At the beginning of the First World War, X-ray machines were only available at the larger hospitals located some distance behind the front lines and where soldiers were being treated for wounds prior to being evacuated home. Curie designed the first *radiological car* which contained an X-ray machine and photographic processing equipment so that army field hospitals could use X-rays in diagnostic investigations. The vehicles were fitted with a dynamo so power to drive the X-ray machine could be delivered by the cars' engine.

Marie Curie Mobile X-ray unit.

The Union of Women of France gave Curie enough funding to manufacture the first radiological car which was used in 1914 at Marne. Thanks to the union a further twenty cars fitted with X-ray equipment were donated, but Curie also needed trained radiographers to operate the vehicles, so she recruited women for the job. She trained over 150 women to become radiographers. In addition to the mobile radiology cars, Curie was also responsible for the installation of more than two hundred X-ray facilities in the field hospitals located behind the battle lines.

Some of the female X-ray workers were injured during the conflicts but they also suffered from the effects of exposure to the X-rays. Because of the urgent need for the mobile X-ray cars, there was no time to perfect safety procedures, however, Curie later wrote a book about X-ray safety drawn from her many wartime experiences. Her intervention led the way to mass radiography units which travelled around the country providing chest X-ray facilities in post-war Britain and this helped many of our ancestors in the early diagnosis of tuberculosis.

Surgical instruments

Maybe your ancestor was a surgical instrument-maker, perhaps not solely following that trade but trading as a blacksmith, cutler (cutlery-maker) or a maker of mathematical and other scientific instruments. Many would have been unaware of the impact they were having on the progressive improvements to medicine, people's health and well-being. Surgical and dental instrument-makers had their own occupational classification in the 1911 and 1921 censuses.

Surgical instruments have been manufactured since ancient times. The earliest surgical instrument-makers were probably the users themselves who fashioned flint-edged tools and adapted reeds and other hollow stems for crude medical or surgical purposes. Trephines (a type of saw) for performing round craniotomies (removal of part of the skull) were used by medieval healers to release evil spirits and alleviate headaches and traumas caused by wounds encountered during battles. Even surgeons and physicians in medieval times developed many instruments including scalpels, lancets, tweezers, forceps, probes, dilators, tubes and arrow extractors. Amputation sets originated after the Renaissance. Throughout the Middle Ages and the Renaissance, the development of surgical instruments continued and a whole range of instruments exclusively for surgery were invented.

Before the seventeenth and eighteenth centuries, instruments were made mainly by armourers, blacksmiths, needle-makers and razor-makers, but in the seventeenth century silversmiths and cutlers began to take over. Decoration of the instruments became important when ivory and tortoise-shell replaced wood and horn.

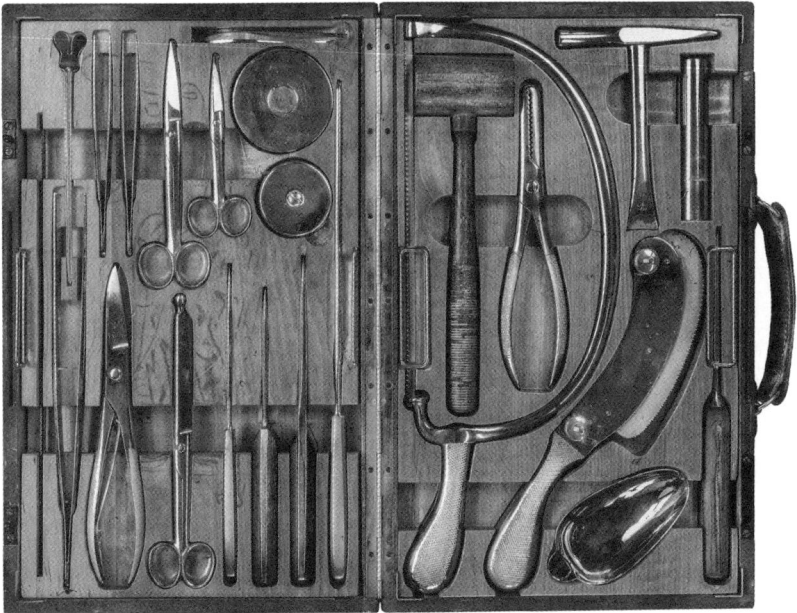

Surgical instruments in wooden case.

However, the occupation of surgical instrument-maker was not really common before 1800 but the *London Tradesman* of the 1740s suggested in a recruitment drive that the trade was a good choice for those for whom no special strength was needed and that working conditions were pleas-ant. Most instruments were subsequently supplied in sets for a particular surgical function. However, it was not until the advent of anaesthesia and surgical antiseptics that many more surgical instruments were invented. New surgical procedures perfected in the Victorian era required new specialist instruments. Materials including stainless steel, titanium and others became available and were used to manufacture the new instruments.

Historically, a surgeon used or adapted a common tool to use when operating on a patient; this could include tools used by butchers, woodworkers or tools used by leather or metal workers. It was shown during the late Victorian era that human blood actually corroded instruments and that sterilization of surgical instruments tended to cause many materials to deteriorate or cause them to harbour bacteria.

Notable British instrument-makers include John Weiss and Archibald Young who was a cutler. Other instrument-makers, however, made their contribution by interpreting the ideas of the surgeon. British surgical instrument-makers have not, on the whole, been very innovative in the design of their products. There are exceptions but in general the typical surgical instrument-maker seems to have been very conservative.

The trade was at its height in the early nineteenth century. Most sizeable towns had one or more amongst its tradesmen. There was also a thriving export trade to British colonies and a high demand from the military and navy medics. The craft of making surgical instruments evolved over the years from being an offshoot of the trade of domestic cutler or blacksmith to a skilled specialist manufacturing occupation. In London alone in the 1890s, there were nearly one hundred surgical instrument-makers listed in the London Post Office directory.

CONCLUSION

Reaching the conclusion in any book is similar to arriving at one's destination after a long journey – and what an experience this has been so far. In this first volume we have met many different medical practitioners, visited a variety of medical establishments and experienced medicine through the ages.

We became acquainted with wise women and witches, dabbled in astrology, bumped into quacks and apothecaries, debunked myths, walked the wards in Crimea with the Lady of the Lamp, Florence Nightingale and assisted Marie Cure in her mobile X-ray vehicles on the battlefields of WWI. We volunteered with the Red Cross and perhaps had to visit a barber-surgeon when we had toothache.

Back on home soil, we have been apprenticed, enrolled, certified and registered as we studied and trained with doctors and nurses in many educational institutions and we learned how medical care became more prioritised and organised over the centuries. We've been cloaked and gowned as we observed early operations including crude amputations … what excruciating pain that must have been!

Therefore we hailed the pioneers for their inventiveness, laughing with Davy as he discovered nitrous oxide, praised Pasteur and Lister and rejoiced at Fleming's Petri dish with its growth of mould – the basis of penicillin. Perhaps the body-snatchers did the medical professions a favour all those years ago when they sold their booty for illegal dissections.

During our journey we visited many different kinds of hospitals; we peeped into almshouses and selected herbs and flowers with the monks in monasteries, and called on workhouses and poor law infirmaries to see how everyone was doing. We sympathised with those who suffered from the Black Death, smallpox and other devastating epidemics which hit the country through the ages. We also assisted various practitioners with the preparation and dispensing of drugs and medicine to those that were in need.

We witnessed new hospitals receiving donations, being funded, built and equipped – from specialist institutions and cottage hospitals to hospital ships. We marvelled at the inventiveness of more and more precision tools so that doctors could see inside the body which helped them form a diagnosis and transformed procedures.

All in all, this has been a fascinating journey through medical time from the earliest monasteries to the more modern hospitals of today. We salute all those famous medical pioneers we met who persevered and worked so hard and made such huge advances in every medical field. We've come a long way from herbs, flowers and potions to vaccinations, penicillin, X-rays and chemotherapy.

Where will our medical journey take us next? In volume two, we shall read about diseases we've probably never heard of, let alone the obscure cures and treatments given from leeches to pectoral balsam. We shall examine diseases specifically associated with work and how accidents could happen. And we shall delve into epidemics and hereditary diseases.

So … wash your hands before you start volume two!

If you have only read this volume, then now is the time to read volumes two, three and four to complete your journey through the lives of the ancestors and the health care available to them.

LIST OF ILLUSTRATIONS

17. Amputation cartoon – Colour process print after J A Faivre 1902. Wellcome Collection. Public domain mark

18. Memorial plaque John Williamson – Photograph ©Suzie Woodward

19. Edward Jenner – Oil painting by E.E. Hillemacher, 1818–1887. Wellcome Collection. Public domain

20. Louis Pasteur – Photogravure after L E Fournier. Wellcome Collection. Public domain mark

21. Joseph Lister's steam spray – The Wellcome Collection. Public domain mark

22. Early contact lenses – with permission from www.contactlenses.co.uk/

23. Doctor anaylysing X-ray – Shutterstock

24. Marie Curie mobile X-ray unit – Photographer unknown. From a "Petit Curie" mobile x-ray unit, 1914

25. Surgical instruments in case- Shutterstock

LIST OF APPENDICES

1. Early medical training dates and establishments

2. Discovery of drugs in the nineteenth century

3. Dentistry timeline

4. Nightingale training school records

5. Miscellaneous nursing records

6. Training ships and the River Ambulance Service

APPENDIX 1

EARLY MEDICAL TRAINING DATES AND ESTABLISHMENTS

The following list indicates when and where early medical training began.

1123 – Medical training facility at St Bartholomew's Hospital, London

1497 – Formal medical training at University of Aberdeen

1540 – Medical school founded at Cambridge University

1546 – Medical teaching at Oxford University

1561 – Medical apprenticeships at St Thomas' Hospital, London

1693 – Formal teaching at St Thomas' hospital, London

1726 – Edinburgh University Medical School founded

1744 – Glasgow University Medical School founded

1751 – Formal medical school established at St George's

1752 – Medical teaching established at Manchester University

1767 – Medical teaching established at Birmingham University

1768 – Formal teaching at St Thomas' and Guy's hospitals

1770s – Formal medical teaching at University of St Andrews

1785 – London Hospital Medical College founded

1794 – Teaching hospital established by Glasgow University

1825 – Medical school established at Guy's hospital

1824 – Formal medical schools established at Manchester and Birmingham

1829 – 1834 Medical schools established in Sheffield, Leeds, Bristol, Newcastle and Liverpool

1834 – 1839 Teaching hospitals established at various colleges of London University

1874 – London School of Medicine for Women

1897 – Medical school established by St Andrews' University at Dundee.

APPENDIX 2

DISCOVERY OF DRUGS IN THE NINETEENTH CENTURY

In Victorian times, some drugs were available from pharmacists on prescription.

The following is a list of some of the drugs and the dates when they were discovered.

1803	morphine
1820	quinine
1830s	santonin
1832	chloral hydrate
1833	diastase
1877	paracetamol
1877	mannitol
1880	phenazone
1885	ephedrine
1890	benzocaine
1895	quinazoline
1887	amphetamine and methamphetamine
1901	drenaline
1906	oxytocin.

APPENDIX 3

DENTISTRY TIMELINE

1685 – The first dental book written in English, *The Operator for the Teeth* by Charles Allen

1764 – First lectures on the teeth at the Royal College of Surgeons, Edinburgh by James Rae

1770 – Porcelain false teeth were invented

1780 – William Addis manufactured the first modern toothbrush

1839 – London Institution for Diseases of the Teeth established

1843 – First *British Dental Journal* was published

1858 – Dental Hospital of London opened the first training establishment for dentists in Britain

1859 – Opening of first dental schools in Britain

1860 – First licences in dental surgery awarded by the Royal College of Surgeons of England

1878 – First British Dentists' Act

1879 – First dental register

1880 – British Dental Association was founded.

1901 – The first dental degree was awarded by Birmingham University

1921 – Dentists' Act: only registered dentists were permitted to practise.

APPENDIX 4

NIGHTINGALE TRAINING SCHOOL RECORDS

The records of the Nightingale Training School are deposited with the London Metropolitan Archives and include the following:

- agreements with the Nightingale Fund Council
- regulations
- reports
- matrons' correspondence and papers relating to the Nightingale Collection; the British Nurses Association, the College of Nursing, and the British College of Nurses
- staff administration
- school buildings
- registers of probationers
- prospectus and syllabus of training
- probationers' duties and timetables
- lecture notebooks
- ward diaries
- examination papers and certificates
- Florence Nightingale's addresses to probationers
- address to probationers by Mrs Wardroper
- accounts
- letters, diaries etc. of Nightingale nurses
- Nightingale fellowship papers
- printed material.

The Nightingale Training School admissions registers cover the period 1860–1920 and include:

- dates of admission and/or transfer to St. Thomas' Hospital
- place of origin
- name and age
- marital status
- religion
- date of appointment
- person recommending
- assessment of sobriety and truthfulness
- monthly assessments of nursing skills
- details of any absences from duty.

Other significant school of nursing records are held by King's College London Archives:

- King's College Hospital School of Nursing, 1885–1998
- Dulwich Hospital, 1917–1967
- St Saviour's Infirmary, [1890]-1931
- Lewisham School of Nursing, 1897–1981
- other nursing records from hospitals into the mid-twentieth century.

APPENDIX 5

MISCELLANEOUS NURSING RECORDS

St John's House – Anglican Nursing Sisterhood

These records are held at the London Metropolitan Archives:

- minutes 1847–1920
- annual reports 1850–1918
- superintendents' reports and diaries 1849–1885
- correspondence 1849–1908
- subscription books 1852–1913
- baptism register for the Battersea Maternity Home 1886–1892
- admission registers 1849–1865
- register of nurses sent to private homes 1849–1855
- register of probationers 1850–1910
- registers of nurses 1882–1919
- register of midwives and monthly nurses 1886–1892
- register of applications for training at St John's and St Thomas's House 1919–1929
- registers of nurses for private duty at St Thomas' Hospital 1933–1944.

Queen's Nursing Institute Roll of Nurses

The Queen's Nursing Institute Roll of Nurses for the UK and Ireland 1891–1931 can also be searched on Ancestry. The records contain the following details:

- name
- date of birth/age
- date of appointment
- where they were educated.

Nursing Records held at the Wellcome Library

Other associated records useful in genealogical research are held at the Wellcome Library including:

- establishment of Queen Victoria's Jubilee Institute
- minutes of council and committees
- records of nurses
- badge awards and other ceremonies
- training and education
- Queen's Nurses' Magazine and successor titles
- relations with district nursing organisations, England and Wales
- district nursing overseas
- records of the Institution of Nursing Sisters
- records and histories of district nursing associations.

APPENDIX 6

TRAINING SHIPS

The Metropolitan Poor Act 1867 meant that the unions and parishes covering London became part of the Metropolitan Asylums District managed by the Metropolitan Asylums Board. The board's initial responsibility was to provide specialised accommodation for fever and smallpox patients, certain types of mental cases, and sick children with long-term ailments or those convalescing.

The board also established the training ship system in 1875 which provided naval training to pauper boys aged up to the age of sixteen, as well as establishing children's hospitals for those suffering from eye, skin and scalp diseases, those who were deemed educationally sub-normal and those who required long-term nursing or convalescent care. The board also developed smallpox and fever hospitals, smallpox hospital ships, the River Ambulance Service and tuberculosis sanatoria. As a result of the efforts of the Metropolitan Poor Act, more infirmaries were built nationwide.

The New Poor Law of 1834 meant that many more paupers entered the workhouse system because forms of outdoor relief were no longer allowed. The increase in admissions resulted in overcrowded workhouses and the Poor Law Board needed to find additional places to accommodate new admissions. They accomplished this by sending pauper boys to training ships.

These ships were generally moored on the rivers Thames or Medway and the unions could send pauper boys to the ships when they were twelve years old; they generally remained on board until the age of seventeen. The regime on board meant that the boys learned how to wash and mend clothing and how to keep their personal areas clean. They also learned to make sails and ropes, to repair sails and other skills necessary for seamanship as well as undertake schoolwork and learn to swim. The primary role of the training ships was to prepare boys for entry into the Royal Navy or the Merchant Navy with the idea that it would prevent them from becoming a burden on the poor law system. Keeping the boys out of the workhouse system and generally off the streets proved to be really beneficial.

Three of the trainings ships were specifically aimed at pauper children – TS *Exmouth*, TS *Warspite* and TS *Goliath* under the auspices of the Marine Society. TS *Goliath* was operated by the Forest Gate School District between 1870 and 1875 when it was moored off Grays. In 1876 TS *Goliath* was completely destroyed by fire killing twenty-three on board. The fire was caused by a paraffin lamp, which although contrary to regulations was somehow allowed on board. At the inquest it was reported that the boy who dropped the lamp tried to douse the flames by flinging his clothes on the fire and he then sat on them until he was burned himself. After TS *Goliath* was destroyed she was replaced by TS *Exmouth* in 1877 managed by the Metropolitan Asylum Board. TS *Warspite* was moored off Woolwich and again held around 500 boys. It was destroyed by fire in 1918 and the offenders were sent to a reformatory.

Accommodating 500 boys on each training ship was considered by the poor law authorities to be about half the cost of keeping them in the workhouse system. Each boy had his own hammock and was expected to help maintain a clean and professional environment. The system was also a good way for boys to learn skills that would help them obtain a career in later life. Training ships were valuable assets to the Poor Law Board and various guardian reports indicated that the boys themselves, as well as their parents, were happy because it avoided the stigma of becoming a workhouse inmate. Some of the ships were established as Industrial School training ships. Each of the ships had its own infirmary for the treatment of the sick, but life for the boys was generally healthy with attention given to their physical development.

If your ancestor was on board a training ship, there are various records that can help with your research but surviving records vary for each type of ship. Researchers should begin by checking the local archive where the ship was moored. Some records include entry registers which will include personal details and the circumstances of admission. They may also show where the boy went to on completion of his term of service, why he was admitted to the ship, his age and ability on completion.

The River Ambulance Service originated in 1884 mainly to convey smallpox patients from riverside diagnosing stations to the smallpox hospital ships lying in Long Reach, near Dartford. The wharves in Rotherhithe, Blackwall and Fulham were used as receiving and diagnosing places. The fleet of ambulance ships began with just four paddle steamers – *Red Cross*, *Maltese Cross*, *Albert Victor* and *Marguerite,* and in 1894 the fleet was enlarged by the addition of *Geneva Cross.*

The smallpox hospital ships were replaced in 1904 by the Long Reach and Joyce Green Hospitals which were adjacent to the river and continued to be served by the River Ambulance Service. Rotherhithe was the headquarters of the service. The records of the River Ambulance Service form part of the Metropolitan Asylum Board's collection held by London Metropolitan Archives.

GLOSSARY OF MEDICAL TERMS

accoucher	a male midwife
apothecary	issued medicines prescribed by doctors
bedesmen	resident of an almshouse and paid to pray for the soul of another
body-snatcher	stole dead bodies to sell for anatomical research
cartulary	medieval register of lands and property
caspie-claws	leg irons
craniotomies	operation involving removal of part of the skull
dispenser	prepared and issued medicines under a pharmacist's supervision
druggist	involved in the manufacture of drugs, not dispensing prescriptions
delirium tremens	often referred to as 'shaking frenzy' is confusion caused by withdrawal from alcohol
epigenetics	the study of heritable traits
grave-robbing	people who stole artefacts and possessions from graves, not bodies
humours	four basic fluids in the body
miasma	foul smells and bad air
ophthalmology	medical speciality that deals with the diagnosis and treatment of eye disorders
ophthalmoscope	instrument for inspecting the interior of the eye
penicillium glaucum	a mould used in the making of some types of blue cheese
pharmacology	the study of how medicines work and how they affect our bodies
physician	medical practitioner diagnosed ailments and illness and wrote prescriptions

plexiglas	tough transparent plastic made of acrylic resin, used as a substitute for glass
quacks	An untrained person pretending to dispense medical advice and treatment
resurrectionists	alternative name for body-snatchers
rubella	German measles
rubeola	measles
surgeon	medical practitioner who performs surgery
trephine	a hole saw with a cylindrical blade used in surgery to remove a circle of tissue or bone
wise women	women who practised herbal medicine and midwifery in medieval times.

BIBLIOGRAPHY

Bynum, W. F., and Porter, Roy, *Living and Dying in London* (Wellcome Institute Medical History Supplement 1991)

Carruthers, G.B., and L.A., *A History of Britain's Hospitals and Background to Medical, Nursing and Allied Professions* (Book Guild 2005)

Fraser, Francis Richard, *The Rise of Specialism and Special Hospitals* (Wellcome Collection 1964)

Jackson, Mark, *The Oxford Handbook of the History of Medicine* (OUP 2011)

Lane, Joan, *The Making of the English Patient* (Sutton 2000)

Mackenzie, Basil, (Lord Amulree), *Monastic Infirmaries* (1964)

Pitt, Rob, *The Craft and Fraud of Physick Exposed* (1703)

Sturdy, Steve, *ed., Medicine, Health and the Public Sphere in Britain 1600–2000* (Routledge 2002)

Wilson, Adrian, *Man Midwifery* (Routledge 1995)

Various journals of the *British Society for the History of Medicine*

USEFUL WEBSITES

Medical Schools in the United Kingdom (Wikipedia): https://en.wikipedia.org/wiki/List_of_medical_schools_in_the_United_Kingdom

Royal College of Physicians Museum – "inspiring physicians" with indexes commencing in 1518: https://history.rcplondon.ac.uk/

Royal College of Physicians Museum – series of research guides, including family history: https://history.rcplondon.ac.uk/collections/our-services/research

Royal College of Physicians of Edinburgh – catalogued archive online at: http://archives.rcpe.ac.uk/calmView/showcase.aspx

Royal College of Surgeons of England – collection of biographies of surgeons at: https://livesonline.rcseng.ac.uk/client/en_GB/lives

Florence Nightingale Medal Recipients – full list online at Wikipedia: https://en.wikipedia.org/wiki/Category:Florence_Nightingale_Medal_recipients

Scarlet Fingers – British Military Nurses with resources about military nursing plus links to other relevant websites: www.scarletfinders.co.uk/

Royal College of Nursing Archive – online copies of its journal: https://rcnarchive.rcn.org.uk/

Royal College of Nursing – its library archives have a family history research guide: https://www.rcn.org.uk/library/archives/Family-history

USEFUL GUIDE TO THE CONTENTS OF ALL VOLUMES IN THE SERIES

Due to the comprehensive nature of this series, aspects of some topics inevitably appear in more than one volume. Therefore, in place of a long complicated index, this useful guide details the contents of each volume, including the appendices. The timeline is the same for every volume.

VOLUME 1 – Medical Practices, Professions and Pioneers

VOLUME 2 – Diseases, Remedies, Epidemics and Accidents

VOLUME 3 – Births, Deaths, Funerals and Mental Illness

VOLUME 4 – Military Medical Care

Timeline
Introduction
Chapter 1   Army medical history up to 1900
Chapter 2   Army hospitals
Chapter 3   Military medicine in the Boer Wars
Chapter 4   Battlefield wounds and injuries in World War One
Chapter 5   Evacuation and treatment of casualties in World War One
Chapter 6   Royal Navy medical care
Chapter 7   Navy medical care at sea
Chapter 8   Navy medical care during World War One
Chapter 9   Navy medical care on land
Chapter 10   Military medical care for troops and POWs in both world wars
Chapter 11   Military nurses
Chapter 12   Commonwealth War Graves Commission
Chapter 13   Exhumations, identifications and records
Chapter 14   Volunteer medics in time of war
Chapter 15   Transition to the National Health Service
Conclusion

Appendices
      1.   Gunshot wounds and injuries
      2.   Facts and figures about Endell Street military hospital
      3.   Navy hospitals
      4.   Scurvy – the nautical disease
      5.   Military medical records
      6.   CWGC records and other military records
      7.   The Wellcome Institute for the History of Medicine

List of illustrations
Glossary of medical terms relevant to the volume
Bibliography
Useful websites
Further reading